the courage to
succeed

Inspiring stories from enterprising women

by

Company of Women

B E L
Learning

Publications by TRIMATRIX
Management Consulting Inc.

This book is published, by arrangement with the authors/ contributors, under the *BEL Learning Publications* imprint by TRIMATRIX Management Consulting Inc.

For information, please contact:
info@trimatrixconsulting.ca

First edition. Published in Canada.

Library and Archives Canada Cataloguing in Publication

The courage to succeed : inspiring stories from enterprising women / Company of Women.

ISBN 0-9735057-8-8

1. Businesswomen--Canada--Biography.
2. Successful people--Canada--Biography.
I. Company of Women

HQ1221.C68 2005   338'.0082'092271   C2005-900824-5

Acknowledgements

Compiling a book like this doesn't just happen; it involves many people…

And, none of this would have been possible without our contributors, who so impactfully shared their amazing stories. We appreciate their honesty and courage in telling it as it is.

Some of the women in the book were interviewed and we thank Pat Atkinson, Anne Day and Christine Desforges for taking the time to meet with people and write their stories.

The book cover has been designed by Christine Desforges and our back cover picture was photographed by Mark Knight and Andrea Nielsen of As It Happens Photography. Thank you for bringing your talent and creativity to this project.

A special thanks to Anne Peace for her ongoing support and for her generous offer to provide personality-type insights to all those involved in the book.

And, to Sheryl Lubbock of TRIMATRIX Management Consulting Inc., thank you for approaching the Company of Women with this great idea for a book. We appreciate your team's expertise in content integration, edit and design, and your partnership as our publisher.

…thank you everyone!

Company of Women

꧁ ꧂

A portion of the proceeds from the sale of this book is being donated to ATHENA, an organization dedicated to inspiring women to achieve their full potential, creating balance and diversity in leadership worldwide.

꧁ ꧂

Table of Contents

ℵℵ ℭℜ

ꠍ ꠔ

Welcome

When we first talked about doing a book, which reflected the stories of the women who are part of the Company of Women, our dilemma was who we could call upon as there are so many fascinating women in our group with inspiring stories to share.

Without fail, as each one was approached about participating in the book, she questioned why she was chosen. Many were sure we'd made a mistake; that we'd got the wrong person. But we didn't think so and, as the stories unfolded, it became clear that we were on the right track. These are ordinary women with amazing courage who have stepped outside of their comfort zone, not only to start a business, but to share their journey with you.

There's no road map to success. Each of us takes a different route and, as you will read, many of us encounter bumps in the road. Some of us take the scenic route and take a little longer to reach our destination; others zoom along and experience instant success. Sometimes we might decide half way that we're headed in the wrong direction and change routes, or make some stops along the way.

Regardless of the journey, having company along the way can lighten the load and, when you share the driving, get you there faster. That's where the Company of Women comes in. We've created a community of women who support each other. We've encouraged women to look at strategic partnerships, to barter their services and find ways to support each other, and it seems to be working.

Some of the women have written their stories themselves, while others felt more comfortable letting someone else tell it for them. Regardless of how the words got to appear on the page, without a doubt there are some common threads in the fabric of these women's lives, and we are sure you will see a pattern that relates to your life too.

Why do people start their own businesses? What causes them to take that leap of faith and start working for themselves? For some of the women, it was a life event that triggered them to take stock, and take control of their own destiny. For others, a personal experience helped them to identify a need and a business opportunity.

Sometimes, it's an employer who catapults one into the world of entrepreneurship as a result of downsizing or dissatisfaction with the work environment. And several of the women turned their passion or hobby into a successful business venture.

A couple of the women have found success in a male-dominated industry, and it's their skill, ability and perseverance that have ensured that they successfully compete in a man's world. While others have had to break stride, just slightly, as they overcome life's hurdles and, as long-time entrepreneurs will tell you, that's all part of doing business. How you cope with the challenges that come your way – the bumps in the road – much determines outcomes.

One common thread throughout is how, as women, we are able to reinvent or evolve ourselves.

We can transfer the skills we developed in running our homes and raising our children into sound management practices. We've learned how to repackage ourselves and take on different roles, and when it's a stretch, that's when we learn and grow the most.

It's been found that women are often very successful in running their own businesses. They may not take as many risks as men, but they do their homework and intuitively know how to juggle the different tasks involved, a key skill for any budding entrepreneur.

As you read these stories, we hope you find the inspiration, motivation and courage to pursue your dreams and achieve your vision of success. And, we hope that you will benefit from the lessons we've learned along the way.

Anne Day

Founder, Company of Women
Author and Editor
the courage to succeed

ဆ ဩ

ඩ ඥ

Getting Started

ඩ ඥ

*"With no role models or examples to follow,
I crossed my fingers, bought canned food
by the case and forged ahead."*

Christine Desforges

All I Ever Wanted

Christine Desforges

I was a thirty-year-old, newly separated, single mother of five-year-old Jaclyn. Outside of child support, my only source of income was my teeny-tiny home-based desktop publishing business. I was feeling the crunch. I had worked only part-time since my daughter was born, and the lion's share of our income had just walked out the door.

My fiscally responsible, dental-plan-loving side screamed, "GET A JOB! A good one, with benefits... and a pension plan!" I did the arithmetic – child care, transportation and other job-related costs would leave little of my pay for living expenses. And I feared that working the nine-to-five grind would exhaust me and leave little energy for my daughter at the end of the day. But the deciding factor was Jaclyn herself. She clung to me. We had just come through a very difficult year and we needed time to heal, adjust and rebuild a new life together. I simply could not leave her, even for forty hours a week.

Still, I felt torn. She needed me at home, but I needed money to feed, clothe and house her. I had to find a way to be primary caregiver and breadwinner both, and make a stable and balanced life for the two of us. I had to grow my business into a source of real income – dabbling time was done. I decided I would work from home until I went broke and needed to find a 'real' job.

That decision became my business plan. Pessimist that I was, I estimated I would be filling out job applications within six months. With no role models or examples to follow, I crossed my fingers, bought canned food by the case and forged ahead. Little did I know that my business would indeed grow, and five years, not months, would pass before I'd decide to take a job – and then only on a part-time basis.

First, I asked my existing (two!) clients for more work. As the workload increased, I stumbled upon my niche – overnight and weekend service. No one else could match my turnaround time, so it made good business sense for my clients to use me. Typesetting jobs began to roll in through my fax machine during the day and artwork orders appeared at my door each evening. I provided accurate proofs and charged reasonable rates. My clients were happy to pick up finished projects each morning and I was thrilled to be earning money at my computer as my daughter slept.

I called former co-workers to offer my services, and slowly my client list grew. I also volunteered my skills, both to give back to the community and broaden my social circle. Not only did I contribute to good causes, but more paying work came my way through new friends and acquaintances. My six-month deadline passed without fanfare, and still I had no need to get a 'real' job. I was delighted.

As the business grew, so did the challenges. If I wasn't careful, my work and my personal life became enmeshed. Boundaries between the two were difficult to maintain at home. At times, I felt guilt when I became immersed in work. I worried that Jaclyn was seeing far too much of the back of my head. I also had to carefully manage an unpredictable income, always preparing for the famine in the midst of the feast. As much as I love solitude, sometimes I felt isolated and lonely working solo. But the benefits of being home-based far outweighed any drawbacks.

With my one-line business plan, I somehow created the best life possible for both of us. Chicken pox and school vacations never caused even a ripple of child care stress; Jaclyn simply stayed home and we both slept in. During the summer months, we spent lazy afternoons at the public pool. I escaped office politics and slippery commutes on snowy days. I worked hard, usually seven days a week, but I got to raise my little girl through the toughest part of her life. And Jaclyn got to keep her mom close by.

She is now in grade 11 – happy, healthy and as balanced as any sixteen-year-old can be. When we talk about that time in her life, she remembers climbing snow banks on wintry nights, eating macaroni casserole at the kitchen table, and quitting Girl Guides at her very first meeting. I still have no benefits or a dental plan, but there I am, in every one of those memories. For her, and for me, that is all I ever wanted.

This contribution is ©2005 Christine Desforges, and is used with permission.

ಐ ಒ

ಖಾ ಞ

Pursuing Your Passion

ಖಾ ಞ

"At the age of 70, she had a poem published and I remember the look of satisfaction on her face. I love it when I hear of older women still achieving, like the one I read about recently who at the age of 96 just published her first book by herself. Wow, that shakes our concepts of what we can all do."

Janee Niebler

Lorraine's Love Story

Lorraine Green

Lorraine describes her business like a love story, with the chapters of her personal and business story very much intertwined. To her, there was her life before the business and a first marriage gone wrong, and then her life with Lorraine's Pantry and a loving relationship with second husband, Rod. With all her passions aligned, life has now brought her the success and happiness she deserves.

Lorraine grew up in Montreal, in a strict and loving Italian family, with a mother who had to work outside the home to make ends meet, and a father who was an alcoholic. "I grew up scared of everything and would turn inside myself and escape to my books, because you never quite knew what would happen next with my father."

"Back then there was no way that my mother could have left, so she worked hard to hold her family together," explains Lorraine. And so with two sisters and a brother at home, Lorraine started cooking for her family when she was 11, and discovered a passion that would last her a lifetime.

When she first left school, Lorraine accepted a part-time summer job with her local bank, and ended up staying twenty-three years. In the early days, she worked as a clerk posting and filing payments and within six months, was promoted to teller, earning the princely sum of $4,000 a year.

Lorraine married early but it did not work out. Like her father, her husband was an alcoholic, and Lorraine recognized that she was being pulled back into the same dark mire she'd experienced growing up. And, after ten years, they separated.

Meantime, she worked her way up the ranks and was involved in some interesting projects, including the move from manual to computerized systems within the bank. In this position, she was required to travel from branch to branch ensuring all the training and documentation was in place to bring the staff into the new, technology-driven world of banking. She also met her now-husband, Rod, who also worked for the bank.

When Rod was transferred to Toronto, it wasn't a foregone conclusion that they would transfer her too. She had to make a sound business case on the advantages of sending her to Toronto as well, and fortunately the company agreed. For a year she was able to work on her own, without too much supervision from head office. "It was really my greatest year in the bank. I had so much freedom in the job and I loved it," shares Lorraine.

After that year, she moved on to Human Resources. Then in the mid-'80s, it all changed. As a result of downsizing, Lorraine now had the upsetting task of working out severance packages for over 60 of her colleagues and peers. "I knew these people. I had worked with some of them for over twenty years," confesses Lorraine, "and the job was starting to take its toll on my health. I had headaches, I wasn't sleeping."

While Lorraine was able to secure a transfer, the job wasn't fun any more. "There just wasn't the same atmosphere. People were worried that they were going to be next," she observes, and she decided to leave. Torn between her love of books and her passion for cooking, Lorraine knew she wanted to start a business, either a bookstore or a catering business, and she opened Lorraine's Pantry in 1987.

Eighteen years ago, there were few choices for fancy appetizers, and so Lorraine decided to introduce her own line of hors d'oeuvres. She made up some samples, practiced her speech in front of the mirror and, with her stomach in knots, nervously set off to sell her products to local gourmet stores.

She got her first order straight away. "He wanted 36 dozen within two days," chuckles Lorraine, "and asked if I could deliver. I told him no problem, and cooked non-stop in order to make the deadline." From there, she developed a one-page menu of meals that she could prepare, and managed to make $10,000 in that first year.

> Do not compromise yourself or your products. Always be ethical in all your dealings, not just with clients but with suppliers too.

Today Lorraine offers over 630 items, from as she says "Soup to nuts." Self-taught, Lorraine is always improvising on recipes, adding her own variations and special extras to make her food appealing and appetizing. She's also been recognized for the quality of her food and service, winning Service Provider of the Year in 2000 and voted Best Caterer in town for eleven years in a row.

With over 1,000 clients and 20 staff who help her serve the food, she still is the only one who cooks. "I like to be in control," she admits. However, 'Mr. Lorraine' (a.k.a. Rod) has been known to chop a few onions and he is Lorraine's biggest fan and support. "He does all the deliveries and bookkeeping. We really are a team, both at work and at home," advises Lorraine.

She also recognizes the influence that her mother and mother-in-law have had on her. "Both were such independent women, raising their children during difficult times, and with such a strong sense of family and work ethic."

Working hard has certainly been a prerequisite to running this successful catering business. "I was surprised at how much physical stamina it takes – from the grocery shopping, to standing in front of a kitchen counter preparing the food, to serving it at events."

> Get involved in the community. I was so busy building my business that I did not recognize the value of giving back and getting involved sooner.

But it has been her passion that has kept her going. "It's important to love what you do," she advises, "but know that it can change and evolve, and when it does, you need to revisit what you are doing from another angle."

And Lorraine is still evolving. She knows she won't do this forever and has dreams of starting a cooking school for young people, creating a cookbook, and even taking some cooking lessons in Tuscany.

No matter what, you get the sense that Lorraine has found her love and passion and, while the ingredients may change, she has the recipe for success.

The Square Peg

Mary Ann Matthews

Ten years ago my life altered radically. It all started with the gentle urge of wanting to take a 'silly' little course. Nothing to hurt my brain. Nothing to tax my mental abilities. Just a night out. Just a new learning experience – an experience that was to change my life.

The course was about the analysis of one's handwriting and the personality traits we reveal through our own graphic movement on paper. Within three hours, my entire world changed...

At the time, I was the in-house recruitment co-ordinator for a major real estate developer, beginning to feel more and more like a square peg in a round hole. A lot of things about my career and my business environment were irritating me. I really wasn't enjoying my life very much until the world of handwriting analysis unfolded before my eyes.

I trained and achieved my certification as a Graphoanalyst (CGA) and started using handwriting analysis as a tool in the employee selection process. Actually, I thought I was pretty hot stuff! I was the only recruiter in the GTA (Greater Toronto Area) that was a recruiter AND a certified handwriting analyst! I had a new lease on life! I was going to knock 'em dead!

To my shock and dismay, many of the senior hiring authorities thought that I had gone over the edge. They thought graphology was voodoo and had no place in corporate Canada. To be fair, there were a few who knew what a powerful tool I had. "Better than a lie detector," said one authority.

Nonetheless, my ego was hurt by the attitude of the majority. I was avoided and, in some circles, shunned. Many thought I had turned into a psychic! So the square peg began to feel more and more uncomfortable.

Shortly thereafter I became the CEO, Founder, and Owner, CCaBW (Chief Cook and Bottle Washer) of Matthews Consulting Services. "Ah, the freedom of being self-employed." I found myself shouting. "I can do your recruiting for you and/or teach you how to do it! And the best part is, I'm a handwriting analyst – I can tell you immediately what it's going to take you three or four months to find out about that new employee of yours!"

I hadn't learned my lesson. I realized that the attitude and perception of handwriting analysis wasn't limited to the corporation I had just left. It was shared by the majority of business owners and representatives. So my infomercial was altered to end with "… oh… and by the way (and this in a whisper)… I am also a handwriting analyst." Clearly my ego and optimism had a long, long way to go. I was still concerned about what others thought about me. I was not living my passion. The square peg continued to exist.

As a self-employed entrepreneur, I quickly came to realize that there is freedom… and there is freedom. Having a home office business meant a commute of two seconds, not two hours. I could start and stop working whenever I wanted! No more nine to five stuff! Now, that's freedom!

Becoming my own accounting department, securing health benefits and insurance plans, and adjusting to getting paid only when the cheques arrived proved to be a very different kind of freedom. The hours of nine to five were replaced with 24/7!

There were times when I would hold my head in my hands and wonder what I had done. I had traded security for freedom. Whatever was I thinking? I could have continued to adjust to the corporate world. The square peg could have compromised. But no, I would mutter to myself derisively, I had to follow my passion! In retrospect, I became very good at beating myself up verbally. I would even throw in the fact that my passion was so unique that few, if any, would accept its validity. What a failure I was! I needed to do a lot of work on myself to change my self-image.

Just over two years ago, I stood up at a networking event and announced, "I AM a handwriting analyst." I even had an edge to my voice! It had taken me eight years to grow through the challenges of dealing with my negative self-talk, of scepticism, of being ostracized for daring to have a passion for a profession that is definitely outside the box. I even changed my company name to handwriting.ca. It felt good to say courageously to the world, "This is who I am. Take it or leave it."

This growth didn't happen overnight. Let me assure you that there are still moments of being scared to death. Being afraid, I have learned, is okay. I now understand that there is no courage without fear.

Having a network, a support system, of like-minded entrepreneurs is essential. They don't have to share your line of work, but they have to be people in your life who you can trust. If you ask them a question, they will give you an honest answer. They respect your confidences as you respect theirs. They can encourage you when you are down and bring you back to earth when your feet are not touching the ground of reality. They are bedrock to your personal self-growth.

I no longer fear the sceptics or the ones that think of me as scary. I now enjoy the reaction of those who look at my business card and say, "Oh, you're a CGA!" (In Canada, that's a Certified General Accountant.) When I tell them that CGA stands for Certified Graphoanalyst, some actually do take a step back from me! Many think I'm a psychic (I'm not) and sense that standing too close to me might be detrimental to their mental health.

I have learned how to deal with those who, as soon as they hear I am a graphologist, will dash off a signature and expect me to tell them all about their personalities. Others are certain that because they print, I can't analyze their handwriting (it's graphic movement and yes I can) or are embarrassed because they think that their handwriting is 'messy' (messy has no value to a handwriting analyst) or that their handwriting is impossible to analyze because it changes all the time (it's still you). I have had others thrust a hand in my face, asking me to analyze them (that's palmistry).

My passion also embraces educating the public about the accuracy of graphic movement and how it really can identify our personality traits. Our handwriting is a projection of our personality. The trail of ink that we leave behind on a sheet of paper tells our story.

… and that's the story of the Square Peg.

This contribution is ©2005 Mary Ann Matthews, handwriting.ca, and is used with permission.

Knowledge is Power

Catherine Bobesich

My story is not so much about me but more a story of the power of determination, will and conquering fears – and, especially, about a passion for wellness. These are the traits that have carried over into my business and have allowed me, as a woman, to blend my experiences – both personal and professional.

In 1994, I was a successful entrepreneur in the image consulting field with 15 years experience in this industry. I believed myself to be fulfilled. The complete recipe for happiness, or so I thought, was there for me: a loving husband, a beautiful son, and a comfortable lifestyle in an upscale community. For all I knew at the time, this was how an ideal life journey was travelled. But as the saying goes, "The reason the world is round, is so that no one ever knows what's coming over the next horizon." It's so true.

Suddenly, I was not feeling very well. I thought I must have been overworked and needed to take a few days off. However, my malaise persisted. I went to see my doctor who, with concern, sent me to a specialist. The specialist told me I had ovarian cancer. I needed to be operated on immediately – within two days. I was shocked and stunned. I was afraid. I was 36 years old.

I was told that this operation, if completely done and to be most effective, would mean I would not be able to have more children. I would not accept this. I authorized only the minimum amount of surgery, knowing that the risk I was taking could be fatal.

Two weeks after my operation, I was referred to a naturopath. It was amazing. This individual showed me the potential of my future wellness by introducing me to a series of self-directed therapies: diet, exercise, meditation, yoga, alternative medicine, drug free regimens, macrobiotic cooking. It was as if I discovered an unknown treasure. I began to read voraciously, over 400 books. My whole life became focused on curing myself in a way I never knew existed.

And then... I became pregnant.

My doctors, however, had severe trepidation about my pregnancy. My husband, my family and my friends agonized about my decision to have this baby, but I went ahead and delivered a healthy baby boy. A miracle!

Years passed and I stayed true to my commitment to wellness. My cancer did not relent, and I had to have additional surgeries, but I knew I was destined to become healthy and well. Today I am cancer free. There was a reason and so my new career started!

I am now a businesswoman who advocates that 'knowledge is power.' From my education and my early career in the fashion and design industry, I began to apply my knowledge to helping women become aware of personal health. It was challenging, but so rewarding.

When I started my business I was still ill, I had a son under two and the personal health market was very small. I had to learn everything on my own. Resourcefulness became my mantra. I applied myself to areas that I had little or no knowledge of, like time management, accounting and marketing.

There was no Internet then, no conference calling and no e-mail. I realized that – as a woman in a start-up company – I had to rely on myself and my relationships with other women as mentors to minimize mistakes and help my business grow.

For me, technology was somewhat daunting but I knew that business success depended on mastering change. And, more than anything else, in the early days of my business, I understood that I had to embrace change and be open to possibilities. After all, compared to conquering my illness, any challenge was minuscule indeed.

My business evolved. The marketplace for wellness expanded and I was positioned to expand my areas of interest. My Web site began to draw international inquiries for my services. And slowly, I was able to put together my team of experts.

I had a mentor and, in time, I also began to mentor others. Additionally, working for various organizations and charities gave me the opportunity to learn how to wear many different hats and attain a new set of skills.

My work now is much more whole and complete due to my personal health challenges and my determination to succeed.

While I have received recognition in my community, I think of myself as just an ordinary, everyday woman, whose perseverance and passion for people has got her to this place.

The success of my business has increased my determination to give back. I use my consulting practice to provide women and their families with healthy lifestyle alternatives, and coach them on having wellness in every aspect of their lives. I also provide advice, counsel and encouragement to women facing the obstacles that a serious health issue represents.

Use your life experience, gather wonderful people around you, have a passion for what you do, and stay open to possibilities.

My story, and what has now become my vast experience in natural treatments and therapies, provides help for other women.

My experience as a cancer survivor has defined my business model and life purpose. I am focused on helping women find health and happiness in life.

This contribution is © 2005 Catherine Bobesich, Wellness By Design, and is used with permission.

Excitement is Everything

Janee Niebler

I once had an image of myself in a dream, as a really old lady with long white hair, giving out medicines across a table. This image was particularly clear and somehow prophetic because it was long before I studied homeopathic medicine. I am almost there... now practicing homeopathy for five years, still learning, still growing and still being excited and not quite the really old lady yet. But the white hair is there and has been since I was 28 and the table is there, my desk in my home office.

I have always been in the helping professions. When I was 18, I decided to be a nurse after walking into a hospital to visit a friend who was a student nurse. I knew that I had to do this. My great Aunt Hettie in Maine wrote my mom and said I had 'had a calling.' I never forgot that, because whatever I did from then on, I was so sure inside that I was doing what was essentially me and felt totally right.

To this day, if it doesn't sit right, I may persist if necessary for a while, but always will turn back to this feeling that I trust. Excitement is everything. Whenever I have done something noteworthy, it was something that I was really excited about, from painting an award-winning picture to achieving knowledge in my chosen field. I know this is the part of us that we should listen to the most.

The same thing happened after years of wonderful and rewarding hospital experience. I began studying for a degree in the mid 1980s and taking all the subjects I loved. I was soaking it all in like a sponge and very much enjoyed studying about Buddhism, and the concepts of yin and yang – everything in life yielding opposites that are in balance and harmony. This understanding, along with new discoveries in quantum physics and the wondrous properties of water as a carrier of medicinal information led me to energy medicine: homeopathy.

I knew I had to study this because it made so much sense. The human body is a whole and everything, even emotions, affects all parts of the body. So we cannot isolate problems, and hope for cure if treatment is separated from the whole. Yet, it is no easy task to find a treatment that fits all aspects of disorder in one human being. It takes longer to improve with these gentler medicines, as one attempts to discover the road to a full cure, not just the quick fix.

After years of nursing, the greatest challenge for me was to balance conventional medical treatment, which after all is my background, with homeopathic treatment. I see people carrying the side effects of medicine that they have taken for years, without a clear picture of what is a real symptom and what is a side effect.

In many ways, my generation of homeopaths are pioneers. Often, when people discover a new way of doing things, co-operation of the sceptical and uninformed is a problem. As with other pioneer fields, one often sees suspicion and hears comments, and so explains and educates. Belief in what you do, determination, networking and meeting people face-to-face are the best ways to reach out and make strides forward. People will refer other people. My hope for the future is that there is global co-operation in pursuing and understanding the healing ways of our vast planet. We would all benefit tremendously!

Getting to know your community business owners will create awareness and understanding of complimentary links, and a new network of referrals.

In the years of study, as I realigned my skills, I struggled to balance my family life – my mother nature side and love of my three daughters, attention to my guy… my husband – and still follow my dream. It was more than a dream really. It was something I just had to do.

The main influence in my life, my mother, always wanted to write. She devoted her life to raising children and staying at home – the way of her generation. Then, at the age of 70, she had a poem published and I remember the look of satisfaction on her face. I love it when I hear of older women still achieving, like the one I read about recently who at the age of 96 just published her first book by herself. Wow, that shakes our concepts of what we can all do.

So, if we listen, we know what we have to do in life, to allow our personal excitement to be heard, before we are little old white haired ladies (or men), wondering what happened to our life. Listen to the excitement above all. I don't know how many years I will be able to practice as a homeopath, but for me now, it is a gift and a privilege and I am so proud of myself for listening.

This contribution is ©2005 Janee Niebler, Homeopathy Life, and is used with permission.

Careful What You Wish For...

Andrea Nielsen

It really should come as no surprise that Andrea is a photographer, given that both her parents were in the photographic field too. Yet growing up, while she liked taking photos, she found her work was often under scrutiny by her parents. They were trying to be helpful and show her how to improve, but from her perspective, the joy was taken out of it and so following in their footsteps was furthest from her mind when she left high school.

It was unlikely that she would have pursued the same career as her father, as he was a medical photographer taking photos of medical procedures for educational purposes. While she proudly shares that her parents photographed the first open heart surgery in Canada, to Andrea, this was all a bit gross.

Andrea spent the early years of her childhood in a suburb just outside Montreal, when as she describes it, "I was untimely plucked from the Montreal culture" with a family move to the rural community of Freelton. She was eleven at the time and as a big girl with a French accent, she suffered at the hands of bullies who tormented her right through her high school years.

She left school at 18 and held down three jobs – working in a sports store, delivering pizza and teaching aerobics classes. Andrea jokes, "I earned more money then than I do now." While it was exhausting, she found it fun. However, after eighteen months, she realized that if she was going to get ahead, she really needed to finish high school, and then go on to business college.

"Business college taught me what I didn't want to do," confesses Andrea, "but now that I have my own business, it's maybe good that I learned a bit about accounting and basic office practices." She held down several jobs but was never very happy with either the work or the pay.

She then went into sales, first cellular phones and then industrial electronics, all the time maintaining her aerobics classes. "It was great! I was paid to stay in shape," she remarks. It was when she was selling cellular phones that she met her husband, with whom she has two beautiful daughters.

With starting a family, she realized that this was an opportunity to refocus, and channel her energies into something that she could be passionate about. Her husband shared something that had been said to him: "The happiest people in life are those who find something they truly love to do, then find somebody to pay them to do it."

Over the years, she had become the official family photographer and would always be found at family events capturing family moments on film. "I really enjoy showing people as they really are, not just smiling at the camera."

So, she decided to pursue portraiture, took several courses and was mentored by other photographers. She started by taking on jobs through friends and family.

She was 26 when she opened As it Happens Photography, which she ran from home for the first six years. It was a fast-paced existence, working evenings and many weekends. "I never knew when the next assignment would come in, so I would take them all. One year, I covered 44 weddings; that's a lot of weekends."

Andrea purchased equipment as she could afford it, and it was only after she had been in business several years that she actually applied for a loan. By then she had a good credit record and her suppliers were supportive. "Maintaining a good relationship with your suppliers is key," she recommends. "They can help you out of tough spots, or not, depending on your relationship."

Andrea has also experienced success in the competitions she has entered and has won provincial, national and international awards for her work.

Two years ago she incorporated the company and experienced even more growth. She has a large studio of 3,000 square feet, in which she has created several imaginative sets that work particularly well for portraits of children.

Not only has Andrea learned a lot about photography, she's become intuitive about relationships. "I can always tell which marriages are going to work, and which won't," she shares. "It's the way the couple behaves before the wedding – whether there is chemistry, mutual respect, communication. Their body language tells me a lot."

It's making people feel at ease and helping to show the real personality of her subjects, that really fuels

Andrea's passion for photography. She takes a creative, artistic approach to her work and is always striving to improve her art.

But while Andrea's business was growing fast, her marriage suffered greatly under the pressure and she is currently separated from her husband. "It's important that your life-partner shares your vision. If they can't, it puts everything out of balance as you try to make both your business and personal lives work," imparts Andrea.

> I strongly believe in mentoring. There is so much to be learned from the people in business. Finding the right mentor is also important.

Managing rapid success, while exciting, brings its own set of challenges. Andrea observes, "The business just took on a life of its own, and grew and grew." She's found that it's not enough to be a talented photographer; you also have to be able to sell yourself and market your services. "I've had to learn to do business differently from the way I started. I delegate more now to other professionals who take on the tasks that have to be done, and which I never got to successfully."

"Time management is my New Year resolution – every year," she confesses. But she's recognized that she needs more balance in her life. As a result, Andrea has become more selective on the type of projects she takes on. She's limited, for example, the number of weddings she will do in a year. And now that her girls live with her one week, and their father the next, she's scheduled her time so that when they are home, she's not working evenings, and when they're not home, she's working full tilt.

> *I've made a point of taking on co-op students from college, and I have them do every job in the studio, so they know all that is involved and that every aspect of any business is important.*

What's next for Andrea? She plans to continue her focus on improving and enhancing her artistic endeavours. "I like to stay on the bleeding edge of technology, ahead of the leading edge," she admits. So when manufacturers ask her to test equipment or software before it's launched, she's quick to jump at the opportunity.

You get the sense that this is just the beginning for Andrea. At 37, she's determined to stay true to herself, no longer will she live someone else's version of her life, and she's working hard to juggle the demands of a creative business with the needs of herself and her family. She's learned a lot in the past ten years and as a dynamic, energetic young woman, you know she is destined to succeed.

This contribution is ©2005 Andrea Nielsen, As It Happens Special Event Photography, and is used with permission.

கு இ

૪ૐ ૐ૨

Finding Your Niche

૪ૐ ૐ૨

"In starting a business, you are the one that has to motivate you. You have to push the business ahead."

Angell Kasparian

Listen to Your Inner Voice

Cathy Boytos

Faced with the financial challenges of raising her three-year-old daughter, Kristen, on her own, Cathy Boytos struggled with finding ways to provide a good and balanced life for the two of them. After a twenty-year career in human resources with a large bank, she knew that she did not want to return to the corporate world: the hours (and the commute) were long, the job was stressful, and there would be little time and energy left for her daughter.

Self-employment seemed like a good option, but she wasn't sure where to start. "I had never run a business before, I'd always had a job. I'm not a big risk-taker, and I had a serious conflict between self-doubt and self-confidence. And starting over was hell," Cathy says.

But Cathy had an idea that just wouldn't go away. After her divorce, she had to furnish her new home on a tight budget, and she scouted second-hand and antique stores without luck. She turned to purchasing used furniture and appliances from classified ads in the local newspaper, and was amazed by the quality of unwanted second hand furniture gathering dust in homes. Cathy wanted to make it easy for people to find affordable second-hand furniture. Could she make a business selling upscale furniture on consignment?

The challenges seemed endless. Friends and family said that she couldn't do it. Cathy's ex-husband suggested that she get a job with benefits. At the same time, Cathy's daughter was diagnosed with a learning disability that required getting Kristen help. Money was an issue; money to start the business was an even bigger issue. In spite of the worries, she borrowed against what little equity she had in her home. Terrified that she might lose it all and be unable to support Kristen, Cathy went after her dream with determination.

Finally, Cathy found the support and assistance she needed to bring Trading Places to reality. She met a fellow who listened to her idea and helped her locate a space to rent. "It was like an angel had fallen from heaven and into my life at that time. He supported me 1,000 percent and spent countless hours of his own time helping me get started," says Cathy. In June 2003, Trading Places opened in a 2,000 square foot industrial warehouse, displaying and selling used furniture on consignment.

She sent 1,200 letters to interior designers and advertised in community newspapers. For several days, she sat in her showroom, marvelling at the beautiful furnishings and accessories surrounding her, and waited in vain for a customer to appear. She was beginning to question herself again.

Many weeks later, on a rainy Sunday afternoon, the showroom was transformed. The place was brimming with people as they lined up at the door waiting to discover what bargains might be found. Cathy sums up her personal satisfaction of that day in saying, "Somebody actually bought something; they valued my opinion."

When asked if it felt good to prove her doubters wrong, she replied, "No. It felt good to prove myself right. I feel good about what I do. These were my ideas and I implemented them. And I did it by myself."

Today, Trading Places is located in a busy plaza, in an upscale 4,000 square foot showroom, and Cathy has six employees. News of the store has spread through word-of-mouth and most pieces are in and out within two weeks. It is not unusual to see a full-size moving van delivering the contents of a 5,000 square foot home to the showroom.

Cathy has just started paying herself; up until now she's been putting all her resources into building the business and hiring the help that she needs to make it work. She has gained the flexibility that she needs to care for Kristen, and looking to the future with optimism. She is fine-tuning the concept and making plans to open more Trading Places locations throughout Canada.

Cathy Boytos saw a need and filled it. She faced self-doubt and uncertainty head-on, took risks, sucked up her fear and made her dream come true. "I've learned that you need to trust your gut feeling. When something keeps nagging at you, it's time to listen to that inner voice. Next time, I wouldn't wait so long and pay less attention to the nay-sayers."

This contribution is ©2005 Cathy Boytos, Trading Places Home Décor, and is used with permission.

Breaking the Rules

Wendy Buchanan

One of the first things you notice about Wendy is her glasses. They are always unique, look good on her and co-ordinate well with her outfit. In fact, you could say that Wendy is a walking advertisement for her product, because what she sells is glasses – not just any old spectacles – but ones that suit your image and lifestyle. And more, she makes 'house calls' and will come to your home or office, to help you make the best selection.

As a licensed optician and trained image consultant, Wendy has combined her experience and expertise to develop a unique, niche business for herself. After seven years, she has close to 900 clients, of which two-thirds are women, and as more people reach over 40, it is safe to predict that this is a growth industry.

Bringing the service to the client has afforded Wendy the flexibility she needs to work around her two small children. She can make appointments to suit her timetable and usually works a couple of evenings when her husband is available to take on the family responsibilities.

Finding the right balance has not always been easy. Take when her son was born. With a relatively new and growing business, Wendy was afraid to slow down and so she worked hard to keep both the business going and look after a preschooler and baby as well. "I was in fear mode," she confesses, "and you don't make your best decisions out of fear." She ended up exhausted and was forced to slow down.

Like many women, Wendy did not leave school and decide to be an entrepreneur. Her first career was as a dental assistant. Anxious to experience college life to its fullest, Wendy selected her dental assistant course because it was just one year and at a local college. "Not the best reason for pursuing a career," she admits, "but I was young, and enjoyed my social life."

However, even back then, Wendy was not adverse to taking risks or working hard. Unhappy in her dental assistant job, she went to meet a friend of a friend who was an optician, and wound up working for him. For five dollars an hour, she would work in a lab making glasses until midnight, while still working in the dental office during the day.

Recognizing that this might be a more appealing career, Wendy went back to school and completed her two-year training to be an optician and each year has to continue with her education in order to maintain her license.

Wendy will be the first to admit that back then there was a pattern to her decision-making style – instant. When two girlfriends decided to move to Toronto, having no job at the time Wendy moved with them. In the end, they left the city and she stayed, working at different optical companies.

However, she grew tired of the internal politics and felt she did not share their values system. On weekends, she took some image courses, partly to improve her own appearance, but also because she thought she might like to become an image consultant. With a business partner, she decided to venture out and offer image consulting services, with a sideline of helping people select glasses that suited them. But as is often the case in business, it didn't go according to plan, and the frame side of the business grew, while the image consulting took on a lesser role.

This created some friction between the partners, and the business relationship quickly soured. "It was messy, like what I would imagine a divorce to be," shares Wendy.

So in 1998, with all this behind her, Wendy decided to forge out on her own. She grew the business mainly by networking. Word-of-mouth was, and still is, her main form of advertising.

She's also repositioned why we purchase glasses. As Wendy points out, "Glasses are fashion accessories, you may want to have several looks. We don't wear the same shoes everyday, why should we wear the same eyewear?"

She loves working for herself. "I'm not good with rules and regulations. I hate being restricted. This way, I have some control," she laughs.

However, she also recognizes that she's learned some lessons the hard way. "If I had to do it over, I'd probably have a more structured business plan, and get some professional advice. While I had the passion and confidence, I probably would have got here faster."

In 2003, Wendy was nominated for the Woman Entrepreneur of the Year Award – Start Up, which provided an excellent process and opportunity for her to reflect and think back on her business. "I've come to realize that I need to go with my gut reaction and listen to my intuitive side," observes Wendy.

Being around positive people has helped, as has the support of her husband, who gave her the wings and space to grow and develop her business. "Not once has he pressured me about money, especially in that first year when I wasn't making much."

Her mother has also been a strong influence in her life. She had her own store and from working there as a teenager, Wendy observed that customer service is important and that sometimes you have to do the right thing, even if it is not profitable.

What's next on the horizon? Wendy is still working that one out, but don't be surprised to hear that she's recruited and trained some consultants to offer the same quality service. Her challenge will be to clone her warm, bubbly personality because an integral part of Wendy's success is Wendy. She has a way of making people feel comfortable and at ease, so choosing glasses becomes a fun experience.

Whichever way it goes, rest assured Wendy will be chartering her own ship, be it one or a fleet.

This contribution is ©2005 Wendy Buchanan, Perceptions Eyewear Inc., and is used with permission.

Life is GRAND!

Angell Kasparian

I guess I would say I just simply knew. While working on a high school project, I just knew that one day I would live in Toronto and work on Bay Street. While I started at an accounting job, I ended up as the director of the marketing and business development support team for the international division of a large financial institution.

I had what I had set out for... I had a fabulous office; I was travelling a lot, going to New York City almost weekly; I loved the people and everything about my job.

At the same time, I was approaching 40. I had always enjoyed a good meal, loved baking and I admit, I had a soft body. My husband and I were heading off on a vacation. And, here I was, packing a day before we were to leave and realizing that I needed a new bathing suit. The choice in February is not the best and at a size 16, my options were really limited. I must have tried on 20 suits that day and, after almost half a day of looking, I found one.

Then I got on the plane with my pile of magazines and I started reading. I continued my way through them for part of the week then I threw them all away. They all wanted me to lose weight, get killer abs, butt, legs, and arms, show my belly button, and wear heels that no average woman my age was going to wear. Why was this happening? Why am I not okay the way I am? I think I'm pretty good. I have a great family, a good job, a house, and pretty much everything I need. I found this all very frustrating.

After the trip, I started to look around for a magazine, Web site or television program that spoke to me and women like me. I couldn't find anything so this was the start of my 'aha' moment.

Meanwhile, back at work, things were reorganized yet again. Projects had come to a grinding halt and people were being let go in every area... good people too. I knew my days were numbered. This was kind of a scary feeling when I was exactly where I wanted to be. I knew I needed a Plan B.

And, the inevitable happened. I was one of the lucky ones though, I did see it coming. In some ways, I was ready. The key thing was to stick with what I knew. Seven months prior to leaving my job, I had already started to investigate my 'aha' moment.

I had discovered what the average size of women was in Canada and what we liked to do. No surprise to me – the average was a size 14 and we like to garden, bike and walk. We are not all a size six or smaller and we don't flock to the gym. Through my research I determined that at least half of the women in Canada were like me. Why wasn't anyone talking to me or people like me? I thought to myself, I know numbers and I know marketing, how about a business plan to do just that – to talk to women like me. This was when GRAND was born.

The business plan took about three months to complete. I spent a lot of time talking to people in the publishing and advertising industries. While, with my experience, I knew how these things worked – starting a magazine, Web site and television show meant there was so much more I needed to know.

When I was released, I took a vacation and launched my company the next month.

Since then, our Web site was launched, GRANDfashion shows started semi-annually, and GRANDmagazine started publishing a year later. Work is just starting on GRANDtelevision.

It is important to have a network of people to call on for support and guidance, but the most important person is you. In starting a business, you are the one that has to motivate you. You have to push the business ahead. You have to make the calls, book the meetings, send out the information and do the research. It is very much all about you, and that fact should not be taken lightly.

The big things I learned are first, don't be afraid to change direction in life; second, knowledge gained is transportable to just about anything; and third, what's past is past and moving on is the best thing to do.

Working from a home office can be very solitary. I have found this to be the hardest part... keeping motivated when all there is to talk to is the four walls or the dogs. There are good days and bad days, but relying on the support of family and friends is the key.

Equally as important, is taking care of you. Take the time to relax, go on vacation, get your hair done or have a pedicure. If not, a business can consume your life.

Everything I learned in one job was usable in the next and everything I learned in the financial services industry has come to bear in launching GRAND – from developing Web content, print production, organizing events and creating sales materials... the processes are all the same just the content is different.

So keep an open mind if and when life throws the big curves. Take what you know and use it; build on it to create a new success.

This contribution is ©2005 Angell Kasparian, GRAND Enterprises Inc., and used with permission.

Fitting a Special Need

Lucy Vandermeer

Three years ago, I discovered that I have an unusual heart condition. This resulted in the need to have a pace-maker, defibrillator implant. After the surgery, I needed a new bra to go over this 'new lump' in my chest. After going to several specialty bra stores, I discovered that it was very difficult to find a garment that suited my 'special need.'

Even before my surgery, I knew that an improperly fitted bra could cause all sorts of problems. When I worked in a lab I had what was misdiagnosed as a pinched nerve in my shoulder. The muscle spasms in fact were in part due to bra straps so tight that they left grooves in my shoulders.

So when I saw that my local college had a new program for professional bra-makers, it seemed like destiny. Not only that, the program would draw on my extensive experience in sewing, design and drafting. I applied immediately and I was one of the first eight graduates in Canada.

I had sewn as a hobby for many years, as my mother had instilled in me a love of creating beautiful things with my hands. But I didn't draw on these skills right away and when I left high school I worked as a research technician for a large paper company. However, it became obvious very early on that this would be a 'dead end' job, and I went back to school and qualified as a medical technologist.

This training led to several sales positions and I travelled across the country for one of the largest medical diagnostic sales companies. But the stress and demands of this career took its toll and, suffering from burnout, I left. It was then that I started to tap into my creative skills – through making draperies, learning drafting skills and designing kitchens.

I seem to find that each milestone of my life has prepared me for the next, each leading me to this very rewarding career. I am able to design and make beautiful garments that meet the needs of my clients. I provide a service that has been unavailable until now. Ready-to-wear does not meet all needs.

I find working with post-surgical breast cancer patients especially rewarding. Women appreciate the colours and fabric we use to help make them feel good and give them back some of their femininity.

The work is an ongoing learning process... dealing with many shapes, sizes and needs. I am continuing to add to my skills. I have just completed an instructor's course so that I can teach others how to make their own bras. I've been most fortunate to have a mentor in my course instructor; without her hard work, skills, dedication and help I would not be where I am today.

What would I do differently? I still haven't found balance. Starting a new business or career takes many hours of hard work and dedication. I have not taken time to 'smell the roses.' I am now scheduling time for exercise and fun. I suffered from burnout once before and don't wish to do so again.

I feel truly blessed. I have been able to take my hobby and turn it into a rewarding career, one that makes a difference in the lives of women.

This contribution is ©2005 Lucy Vandermeer, Bras by Lucy, and is used with permission.

A Recipe for Successful Delivery

Heather Wilgar

Being an entrepreneur and starting a business with my brother Michael was something I had envisioned since I was 14 years old. It was simply a matter of coming up with the right idea and just going for it.

I was a competitive figure skater growing up and, as such, diet and nutrition were always of vital importance. I had been turned onto the Zone Diet created by Dr. Barry Sears, but with all the weighing and measuring of ingredients I found it quite difficult and time consuming and my solution was to cook a batch of zoned chili every Sunday and eat that for lunch every day.

Monotony makes it hard to stick to a diet. Then one night while watching Entertainment Tonight, Jennifer Aniston was talking about a service in New York that actually delivered a day's worth of meals to her door each morning. I said to my mom immediately if they had that service here in Toronto I would use it. Her response was "Why don't you start it yourself?" and the idea was born!

I was in corporate recruitment at the time, and eventually quit to start the business, which is a meal delivery service that provides three meals and two snacks to clients on a daily basis. We are a healthy lifestyle… delivered.

There were just so many things that we as virtually kids (I was 26 and Mike was 22) simply didn't know about starting a business and without the aid of professionals, we could have headed for trouble down the road. We learned that an accountant and a lawyer are essential to the success of a start-up company.

Prior to our official launch, there were so many issues to deal with. We had all the papers and permits. Pre-orders were accepted on our Web site. We even had a chef to prepare the meals for us, but we needed the hard inventory to get this business going. These items all required money and so we needed to write a formal business plan if we wanted to get financing.

Mike and I ambitiously sat down to write our plan one day on a computer-based program that outlined everything that had to be included. We found ourselves already stuck by the third section when we needed to include costing on so many things and we didn't know what the bottom line would be. Fortunately, our father works for a credit union and was able to obtain a line of credit so we could start our company.

But this may not be as simple for others trying to start a business with just a lofty idea and no business plan to show, so I'd strongly recommend starting off with a solid business plan with projections and targets for the first year of business, as this would have been useful to us as we moved forward through our start-up.

Only two weeks before we were set to begin and we still didn't have a kitchen. Where would we operate out of? You can't prepare meals in your home, and we had exhausted all options with regards to leasing an existing kitchen.

At the eleventh hour, we got the lead on someone that operated a catering company, who would allow us to use his space and equipment, for a nominal rental fee, between 6 and 9 p.m. each day after his staff were gone for the day. Now we were really ready to go!

At the end of our third day of operation, Mike and I were in tears with an uncomfortable heavy feeling; we felt completely overwhelmed with the enormity of what we had undertaken.

After wiping the tears, we hit the road because we did the overnight deliveries for almost the first year of operation with the help of our mom and significant others. We would be out until 5 a.m. and back in the office at 9 a.m. each day, making for a twenty-hour workday.

Two months into the operation our original chef decided that this form of cooking was not for him. But we reconnected with an old friend with a catering business who took over food preparation.

This freed up our time as we were no longer needed at the kitchen every night. We also came up with different delivery strategies, but it was not until we hired a courier service to handle the overnight deliveries that Mike and I were able to live a slightly more normal life. Although we still received calls nightly from the staff.

My relationship suffered the wrath of the new business and sadly ended, but Mike's girlfriend is now his wife, and they can look back on the beginning and hard times they shared. We never stopped to look at what we had created, we always thought of it as not far enough along, not enough clients, not enough money in the bank, not enough...

Today I run the company on my own with the assistance of a virtual assistant who handles all of the administration and sign up of new clients. I have let the courier service go and have retained private drivers with one lead driver who co-ordinates everyone.

> Take the time every now and then to acknowledge your successes, whether it is earning a new client, helping a client reach their goal or reaching a monthly sales target.

My mother is the backbone of the operation as she handles all the books, an unpaid position she has taken on, in addition to her day job.

With the bookkeeping taken care of and the complete automation of our online ordering system, I now have the time to focus on sales and marketing which are vital to the success of any small business.

I am lucky to have been featured on many health television shows, in magazine articles and in all the main newspaper publications in Toronto. This unpaid advertising is extremely helpful for business.

I also send out a monthly newsletter to previous clients to keep them informed of the new things that are happening. This tactic has been quite successful, as it is much easier to win back a previous client than constantly having to attract brand new clients. We also have exclusive contracts with sports clubs organizations and corporate concierge services that all promote our service.

After three years in business, it is easy to look back and recognize that so many people we simply knew have helped or aided in our success in some way or another. Ask for help – ask those you know and those they know!

Ask for help – ask those you know, and those they know!

I cannot even begin to explain how dramatically this experience has impacted my life, and I cannot paint an overly glamorous picture either of what an entrepreneur actually does – which is everything.

We're on the right track now, but it took a lot of work and a lot of help from others to get the company to where it is now. I wouldn't trade my experience for anything, and I love being an entrepreneur and running my own operation. The long hours are so much more gratifying when you are the boss!

This contribution is ©2005 Heather Wilgar, DietDelivery Canada Inc., and used with permission.

ఙ ఞ

৪৩ ৫৪

Taking the Plunge

৪৩ ৫৪

"What's more important, being successful or being happy? For me, the answer is: I'm successful because I'm happy."

Nancy Douglas

Life in the Fast Lane

Nancy Douglas

When I was first asked to write about myself and my transition from corporate executive to professional life coach, I didn't think that I had anything important to share with you.

Why? Because my corporate life was a lot more about corporate than about life. In fact, during my last years in the corporate world, I had no life! I just worked.

I didn't have time to be happy. However, I believed at the time that without my job and everything that went with it, I would have no chance for happiness. How very wrong I was.

For seventeen years, I travelled regularly throughout Canada, the U.S. and Europe. Not that my life wasn't exciting – there were conventions in Hawaii, champagne dinners in France, shopping in Paris and London, speaking engagements in California. But I missed a lot.

So, why did it take me so long to make a change? Fear, I think mostly. When the company where I worked was sold to a U.S. corporation, there were many changes and so began my bi-monthly commute between Toronto and Dallas.

Two years later I was asked to move permanently to the U.S. Wow! How exciting! A green card. More money. More opportunity. I was given two weeks to make my decision. This was the kind of promotion I'd been working so hard for, so why wasn't I packing already? After considerable thought, I realized that I would miss my family, my friends, my home and my cat too much.

I turned down the offer and instead became the corporate spokesperson and began travelling even more. I was a high achiever, received awards, special trips and, eventually, was promoted to vice-president and became a member of the senior executive team.

During this time I purchased my first home. On the night the offer was accepted, I had to meet my realtor after midnight because I was tied up in a business deal. In all the time that I lived there, I never even painted a wall, which given that I was in the decorating industry, is further comment on the pace of my life. My exciting new condo turned out to be a 1,400 square foot walk-in closet with a latch-key cat as its only full time resident.

Then times got tough, really tough. The company was in serious financial difficulty. Now the workload was not only heavy but extremely stressful as well. Then came the merger, closing factories, offices and distribution centres and lay-offs.

I was absolutely exhausted and now I really had no life. So I finally quit, right? No, I didn't. No, I was afraid. Afraid it would be wrong to leave now when the chips were down. Afraid I wouldn't find anything else to do after working for the same company for almost fifteen years. And quite frankly, I was just too tired to contemplate looking for something else. In retrospect, I realize I cared more about someone else's company than I cared about myself.

Eventually I was offered a package. Free at last! I was forty-two years old and excited about life... my life.

I had a roof over my head, money in the bank and a whole year to figure out what I wanted to do next. I was ready to live. I took courses, taught yoga classes and literacy to adults. The world was my oyster and all I had to do was experience it. I had plenty of time to find my next career.

I was going to reinvent myself. And I was going to have fun doing it. But after eight months I still hadn't figured out what I was going to do with the rest of my life. Work wise, I couldn't seem to identify with anything. If I wasn't Nancy Douglas, Corporate Executive, who was I?

Financially, I would soon need a job, but spiritually my soul needed something different. But what? Then one day I received a phone call and was offered a similar position with another company. I hesitated. They offered more money. I was afraid to take the job, but even more afraid not to. Every time I hesitated, they upped the ante.

I felt I had no choice but to go back to the only world that felt familiar to me. I knew I didn't want this job, but I didn't know what it was I did want, so I accepted their offer. But the hours I worked were impossible, so after two years, when my new boss told me he expected me in the office early every Saturday morning, I resigned. I knew my life depended on it.

I was petrified, but slowly I started to rediscover myself. I asked myself what I had truly enjoyed. What gave me the most pleasure and a sense of accomplishment? I remembered that I would often be the one who people would come to for advice – go figure! – the one with no life outside of work was giving advice to those who had. And I was good at it too.

Conversations would start out about work but would usually lead to the 'real' issues. I spent countless hours listening. I seemed to be able to hear what people were saying and intuitively guide them to discover their own answers. It wasn't called coaching then, it just seemed to be what a good colleague, boss or friend would do, and something I did naturally and with ease.

I hadn't paid much attention to this skill, but with the help of my own coach and her questions, questions that I would never have known to ask myself, I soon discovered where my true passion lay. I was learning so much about myself. I began to do some research into this emerging field called professional life coaching and realized that I'd been doing it all my life in between my 'real' jobs.

So, at forty-five, I went back to school. Now four years later, I'm doing what's right for me. I love my work. It's challenging and rewarding and I learn something new every day. I have balance now and a life. I work hard but I also play and I laugh a lot more often. I don't take myself so seriously.

I use all the skills I developed in my corporate years and more. In fact, I feel like I've been in training all my life for this career.

I have a wonderful relationship and good friends. I'm closer to my family. I got a dog. And I've moved and have a home that I've renovated and decorated from top to bottom.

Twenty years ago I aspired to be the CEO of a large corporation, now I'm the CEO of my life. I've often been asked, "What's more important, being successful or being happy?" For me, the answer is: I'm successful because I'm happy.

This contribution is ©2005 Nancy Douglas, Strategic Life Coaching, and is used with permission.

Coffee, Tea or Me?

Marcia Barhydt

My title refers to my career as a flight attendant – wonderful years in my life, during which I saw the world, married, had two children, divorced, kept flying. Finally, when flying was just too physically painful to continue, I obtained a position in the airline's catering office.

This job opened my eyes to a whole new world. I had never operated a computer, had really never worked in an office before and I certainly didn't have much confidence that I could do a good job. But, in spite of my doubts, I did a very good job because I so loved what I was doing. That took me to the end of my thirty-two airline years. And that's when the real changes began...

When I decided to retire and start my own company, I must admit I had no idea what I was undertaking. I'd barely worked in the business world, let alone run my own business. But by finding courses to help with the basics of entrepreneurship, I struggled ahead.

I gathered up all my nerve and dived into something new. It was terrifying, but you never know what you can accomplish until you try. When you have a passion for your business, your passion will make you excel almost automatically. Here are some lessons I learned along the way.

Be prepared to change

I had decided that my business should be about customer service (something I really knew well from my airline days) and I soon decided to be a trainer. I spent three months writing my own training programs and then I began to try to sell my programs to prospective clients. Yikes! What an eye-opener!

After the first round of turn-downs, I was a little less bright-eyed and bushy-tailed; after the second round I was questioning my ability and after the third round I was almost hostile to my prospects – which isn't the best attitude to have when selling!

This new life as an entrepreneur was a huge change for me – I had never worked harder for less money, longer hours and more worry. And with no results! When one method of attack didn't work, I tried a new method – but I had the tenacity to keep trying until I found the method that works for me.

I stopped cold-calling and started networking. Networking became my salvation, both of my sanity and of my success. And it was something I loved doing.

In hindsight, I realize that at first I didn't choose networking groups that were really right for me. But I learned to recognize when a group wasn't working for me and move on to a new group that would be a better fit.

Listen to the advice of others

Listen to others when they make suggestions. Their ideas are gifts. One woman I met suggested that I write and weave my airline stories into my training programs. Well I did, and amazingly it worked; people loved these stories. I never thought my new direction would include writing, but I was flexible enough to give it a try and it was very successful.

Give your time freely to others and you'll all benefit

The way we act and react to our business contacts should be no different from the way we do to our friends and family. Generosity in business, just like in life, will come back to you. Run your business with the morals and ethics that you run your personal life.

I was anxious to become part of some of the groups I joined and volunteering was just a natural extension. Volunteering has led to some good business contacts and even a couple of new clients, but the main reason for volunteering is that we all need to give back to the community that supports us.

Take time to mentor others – I don't mean coaching for money, but simply mentoring to be of help. During my company's five years, I've met many women who were just starting out. And I've eagerly supplied them with contacts and resources that might help them. Mentoring is a warm fuzzy – you feel good doing it and if you enrich your colleagues, they'll always remember your kindness.

It's also important to do freebies – whether this involves a product or a service. Freebies are especially important if they expose you to a new group of prospects, but because it's a generous thing to do, even groups who can't afford you will benefit and they'll be so very grateful of your generosity.

Keep your competition close – close enough to make them your allies

When you meet another person whose company supplies the same products or services as you, don't think of her as a threat. Remember always that you're the only one who has your own personal style. Others might have the same product, but they don't have the same product with your special twist. And becoming close with your competition can result in a joint endeavour that would benefit both of you.

Often, you can help your competition by taking over her excess business from time to time. And you'll both always have a wonderful commonality to help you discuss and plan future activities.

Build a support network

One of the biggest changes that has occurred in my life as an entrepreneur is going from being a very social person, constantly in the public eye, to becoming a home-based business owner. The perils of being home-based are vast, primarily because of isolation. You sit there in front of your computer and discover you have little idea of how others are managing.

I found that changing lifestyles from social to private was a huge adjustment. I felt I was on totally new ground without many resources to help me along the way. This may happen to you also – know that this stage will pass and you'll learn how to adapt a new lifestyle that includes who you were with who you are now.

When I'd been in business for about six months, I started to run into a funk – a period lacking in confidence in my ability. "What am I doing here?"

became my mantra, followed quickly by "Whatever made me think I could make a success at this?" and ending with the terror of "What if they find out how inept I am?" This was not just a temporary attack – I'd often not even turn my computer on for two weeks. And I'd continue to spiral down the vortex of self-pity and self-doubt.

Then I connected with two women who supported and encouraged me. One always managed to give me a pep talk about my abilities to prosper, which led me back to my computer and to my efforts to run my company. Eventually, after quite a few talks from her, I became able to give those pep talks to myself and the more I did, the less often it was needed.

The other, one of the most nurturing women I know, whenever I had a small victory, would always say, "Good for you – I knew you'd do well at that." After a while, I started to believe her and then believe in myself.

Form a mastermind group

These two women are now very close friends and we've now formed a kind of mastermind of three. We meet monthly for lunch and we each take our turn talking about the past month's challenges and upcoming plans and hopes. We each give honest feedback and suggestions to each other and we value each other's advice so much, simply because we trust each other.

When you form a mastermind group, only do it with women you admire, trust and feel totally comfortable. Share everything with them – your good moments as well as your bad ones and really listen to their advice.

Their caring will guarantee suggestions that will benefit you.

I was unaccustomed to relying on others for support and advice. It was a massive shift in approach and attitude for me. When I did learn to accept others' advice, my life was suddenly easier, partly because I felt so much less alone.

Your business is not your life

Everyone talks today about finding balance; I can tell you from experience that it's essential to your success as a business woman and as a person. I suspect, like all new entrepreneurs, you'll spend much, much more time on your business than you ever did on a job – it's natural to want results quickly.

I personally spent so much time during the first two or three years that I ended up getting very sick three months in a row – the last of which ended in a hospital stay. Finally, I realized that some changes needed to be made. I made a decision that I would no longer choose to work as hard as I had been.

Don't be so rigid that you refuse to make changes that result in a kinder lifestyle – don't buy into the super-woman myth. Instead of being mediocre at many things, find whatever way you can to be superb with the few things that are important, really important.

For me, this required a massive change – I sold my house and moved into an apartment where the financial demands on me would be greatly lessened. This also came at a time when my first granddaughter arrived and I knew that I wanted to make changes that allowed me to have enough time to make her a part of my life.

I needed to reprioritize the important things in my life (my health, my family) and see them as more important than my business priorities. It's no longer critical that I work 24/7 because my living expenses are lower and this gives me time to spend on my other priorities.

I found and kept the courage to make whatever lifestyle changes are necessary for me. My business is not my life. When I realized that, I was able to make appropriate changes to include all the other important parts of my life. There is no greater achievement than balance and moderation in all parts of my life.

It's been an amazing five years, during which I've been constantly changing and renewing myself and changing and renewing my direction. Change is good – renewal is outstanding and extraordinary. It is the best possible gift. Embrace yours!

This contribution is ©2005 Marcia Barhydt of Willowtree Customer Service, and is used with permission.

Finding Life's Purpose

Carol-Ann Hamilton

What's your definition of success? By today's standards, my first two decades in business represented the high life. They were the pinnacle toward which we are taught to strive. University professors held out this life as the lucrative reward for enduring five years of studies.

However, I could easily say that twenty-two years employed inside corporations turned me into a physical, emotional and mental wreck. While others might believe I had achieved the North American business ideal, I feel I had attained the height of spiritual despair.

You see, while at the top of my employed earning power, I began a journey to discover and design my life according to a broader reason-for-being. This exploration culminated in a major decision to leave corporate life.

Once I was crystal clear about my larger life mission, it became increasingly impossible to withstand reporting to an unending string of dysfunctional bosses tolerated by toxic organizations.

And so I found myself at a crossroads. Either put up with the abuse or save my soul. Of course, it is not as simple as that. Or is it? For me, the benefits of staying in an untenable situation were eventually reduced to a regular salary, paid vacations and a prestigious downtown location.

Now, you might think, if it was that painful, Carol-Ann, why didn't you call it quits sooner? Ah, there's the rub – one word – FEAR.

Upon reflection, one sure gets used to automatically withdrawing pay from that magic hole-in-the-wall every two weeks. The power of 'golden handcuffs' cannot be over-estimated. Paired with the eternal hope that things will improve by hanging in, this lethal duo chained me to my desk in an almost inescapable grip.

The core of my new business is to make the world a better place by encouraging leaders and employees to build soul-inspiring work environments. My sad experiences have informed my bigger-life purpose.

For five years, I gave workshops, coached and wrote my book on weekends and vacations before freeing myself. I finally needed to impose a deadline, otherwise my dream was at risk because of my fear of leaving the perceived security of employment.

Contrary to the advice books, I went cold turkey – without a roster of established clients, a padded bank account or a solid business plan.

It took sheer guts and iron determination to persevere through a very transitional first nine months, during which we also found out that my husband had some serious health issues. None of which bodes well for a fledgling business venture.

So how do you stand with confidence and trust in your viability when all evidence points to an early close? Why undertake such drastic measures when proven authors counsel a gentler slide into entrepreneurial reality?

The answer lies in my broader life purpose and my need to be a pioneer-visionary, known for inspiration and unyielding commitment to my higher ideals of truth, freedom and integrity.

While still taken aback by how emotionally challenging my start-up phase was, I would not change a whole lot about the original process.

Here are some reflections that may help you...

- Define in detail what your ideal (entrepreneurial) day looks, sounds, and feels like
- Get really clear about your uniqueness (gifts, talents, values, message), what someone else might call your 'brand'
- Describe the qualities and behaviours of your ideal client
- Consider what character traits you will need to draw on in order to succeed
- Adopt an abundance philosophy where you profoundly believe you will prevail
- Check in with yourself on a regular basis to make sure your activities reflect your inner core

Since then, I have found it important to get more focused by examining how new commitments fit with my bigger life purpose. As an unlimited thinker, it is all too easy to spread my precious energy too thinly because so much interests me.

I believe that whether on a global, national or individual scale – hearts everywhere are yearning for spiritual renewal. No more are employees prepared to function as mere cogs in the organizational wheel.

Spirit in the workplace is good for business and good for people. As you build your businesses, remember that generating outstanding profits and nurturing the human spirit are not mutually exclusive, they are synonymous.

This contribution is ©2005 Carol-Ann Hamilton, Changing Leadership, and is used with permission.

ॐ ॐ

Transferring
Your Skills

ॐ ॐ

"I found that the skills I had learned through all my past positions and my personal life could be applied to other things."

Heather Resnick

A Life Long Learner

Teresa Biagi Gomez

"My daughter Sofia could never say a word to me, yet she taught me the most about communication and life," shares Teresa. "She showed me how to look into people, not to just judge them from the outside."

Sofia, who had cerebral palsy, lived a short life. She was six when she died and, for Teresa, Sofia is always present in her heart, and gives her courage. "When I look at the different challenges we've faced, nothing compares to our experience with Sofia. So starting a business, going back to school, and moving to a new country, all pale in comparison," she explains.

And Teresa has done all that and more. Growing up in Mexico, she was raised in a loving family with three sisters, and a brother who, sadly, died when he was six.

Teresa spent most of her childhood living in Mexico, except for a two-year period when the family moved to Switzerland, which she found to be an exciting and positive learning experience. This is where she first had to use her English.

She'd always had creative talents and upon leaving high school, entered the Universidad Iberoamericana in Mexico to study industrial design. There she met her husband, who was taking the same courses and upon their graduation, they got married and decided to take a further degree – but this time in Canada at Carlton University.

They saw this as an adventure, as an opportunity to live in a new country, further improve their English and "to be honest", confesses Teresa, "to be away from our families." So they loaded all their worldly possessions into their Rabbit car and drove to Canada. It took fifteen days and they found their one-year stay to be the start of a bond with Canada. "One of the things I like about Canada is the women. They're not afraid to say what they think; they support each other and show that they care."

When the program ended, they moved back to Mexico and set up their own design studio. They would take a design concept from start to finish, for example: with a furniture corporation, they provided consulting services which included catalogue, product, display, and furniture design.

Recognized within their industry, they were asked to design the logo for the Mexican Olympic Committee. They were also very entrepreneurial in their endeavours and had several business ventures running at the same time. Take the fridge magnets that they designed and developed from their kitchen. The magnets proved very popular and soon their kitchen table became like an assembly line as they worked to fill the orders.

With a distribution system in place to market their magnets, they took on the distribution of other items such as coffee machines and all was going well until the free trade agreement was signed. Then products from China soon took over the marketplace and it was hard to compete with their prices.

At the same time, companies were hitting hard times and the demand for their services declined. Their studio went from eight employees to just Teresa, working freelance to secure contracts as her husband decided to focus his energies on his father's business.

Yet exciting opportunities were still presenting themselves and Teresa found herself first taking courses, and then giving courses to new entrepreneurs and crafters on how to design their product line and then market and package their products. For three years, she travelled to different cities sharing her expertise with local artisans.

> Look inwards and decide what your strengths and passions are and what you have to offer. Research and decide what you will do differently...

Teresa also became somewhat of an artisan herself, when through the World Gold Council she participated in the development of a trend book for the jewellery industry. Little did she know that this would kick-start her own career as a jewellery designer.

"I enjoyed the project so much that I started to make my own models, learning the trade by apprenticing at the bench," shares Teresa.

Moving back to Canada was not an easy decision as it meant leaving her parents, friends and culture behind in Mexico, but Teresa and her husband felt there was a brighter future for their family in Canada.

She devoted her first year to helping her four sons, Rodolfo, Adrian, Julian and Patricio, now 19, 18, 15 and 13 adjust to their new home country. "It is sometimes hard to always speak English," observes Teresa. "There are times when I am really tired, that I forget my English and I just want to think and speak Spanish."

It has been two years since Teresa started her own jewellery design business and she has around 360 different designs. "I've never had a nine-to-five type of profession," she observes. "My most productive hours are usually between 8 p.m. and 1 a.m. It's a quiet time when I can think and concentrate."

A life-long learner, Teresa continues to take courses that will help her master her trade and assist her in growing and building a business here in Canada. However, with two sons now in university, she's realized that her business needs time to mature and that financially, she needs to explore other earning possibilities until it is more established.

> Be prepared to work, work, work and be persistent. There are no standards or timetables for success. You have to use your creativity to make the reality you want.

She has taken a sales position with a large furniture store and sees this as an opportunity to learn more about the sales side of business, which can only further her knowledge of the Canadian marketplace. And in the meantime, like many women, she works at her business on the side.

With her positive attitude, design talents, thirst for knowledge and ability to grasp new opportunities, it is clear that Teresa will succeed in whatever she chooses to do. We're just fortunate that she's chosen to make her home in Canada, as we now have a new design talent in our midst.

This contribution is ©2005 Teresa Biagi Gomez, Designer-Jewellery Collection, and is used with permission.

A Fresh Start

Cheron Long-Landes

If launching a new business means navigating unknown territory, then Cheron Long-Landes has set herself a most challenging course to success. She has not only started a new venture – she has also begun a new life in a new country at the same time. Cheron arrived in Canada only in 2003, bringing with her a passion for textiles and a burning desire to run her own company.

And she's off to a great start. In September 2004, Cheron launched Cheron Dearle Designs Inc., a home decor company which specializes in soft home furnishings – high-quality bedding, throws, cushions and table linens. Cheron designs and oversees production of all her own products and is now in the process of marketing her line to retailers, all the while adjusting to her new way of life.

Though exciting and fresh, it hasn't always been easy. Coming from rural Germany to suburban Toronto means dealing with a culture shock – imagine how confusing the land of the 'double-double' and 'GTA' can be without a handbook. "There's no learning curve," she explains. "It's sink or swim!"

Being new to Canada also means Cheron has no contacts; every call is a cold call. And with no history here, Cheron must pay for all her fabrics and supplies up front. Negotiating discounts also proves very difficult. But these obstacles don't discourage Cheron, she meets each challenge with quiet determination and pluck. Cheron also has a cheering section in her sister, who supports and encourages Cheron at every turn.

As daunting as adjusting to a new country and starting a business seems, Cheron is uniquely qualified to cope. Originally from South Africa, Cheron left home at the age of 18 to train as a dress designer in London, England. In all, she has lived on four continents throughout her life, including a twenty-year stint in Germany. Now she is here to stay. "I feel like I'm just waking up. Canada represents the chance to accomplish what I've always wanted – to operate my own company," says Cheron.

The thrill of that prospect, coupled with a positive attitude, means that she doesn't let the stress overwhelm her – to Cheron, life is all about starting over, again and again. She is inspired by the story of her ex-husband's late father, who lost a leg at age 19 in WW II. Upon returning home, he started over with a successful business, only to lose everything he had built in a divorce. What did he do? He started again. His example feeds Cheron's philosophy that there are no good or bad experiences – each life event contributes to who we are and how well we are able cope.

Her father-in-law also set the example that Cheron hopes to follow in the future with her own company. "His door was literally always open to his employees. He showed amazing respect and support for the people who worked for him," Cheron says. This is the kind of leader she plans to become to her future employees as her own company flourishes.

Cheron has many other plans for that company. She dreams of the first huge order that will mark her entrance into the Canadian home decor market. Eventually, she wants to own her own factory, where she will have more control over the production process, solve problems on the fly and bring all of her creativity to the task. In the meantime, Cheron hopes to find a mentor to help smooth her way into the Canadian market. "I know there are no short cuts, I just would like to avoid the dead-ends and stay on the right path," she explains.

To get there, Cheron has done her homework. She prepared for launching her business by attending a course three days a week for three months, which covered everything from marketing to legal issues to preparing a business plan. Cheron has also joined Toastmasters to help her present herself and her product in the most effective way.

Networking has also been a large part of her life, as she has done the rounds at various groups and become a member of Company of Women in the process. She marvels at the amount of help, advice and information available to entrepreneurs in Canada, and has taken advantage of every opportunity that has come her way. Cheron also gives back to her new community as a registered driver for the Canadian Cancer Society and as a volunteer at her local church.

But she hasn't stopped there. Cheron also works one-on-one with a life coach, who helps keep her focused and positive. "Life coaching has helped me attack the gremlins of self-doubt that can prevent success," she explains. Clearly, Cheron is covering all the bases to achieve her goals in Canada.

Cheron came here looking for a fresh start, and in a relatively short time, she's made unknown territory her home. What would she do differently? Not much, it seems. Despite the challenges, a new country and a new business add up to the life that Cheron always wanted. In many of the most important ways, Cheron has already triumphed.

This contribution is ©2005 Cheron Long-Landes of Cheron Dearle Designs Inc., and used with permission.

Military Lends Backbone to Business

Eva Martinez

Everything happens for a reason – even if at first the reason isn't quite clear to us. I have countless examples of this learned lesson but the most relevant is the one that led to the creation of my company.

Up until 2002, I was enjoying an extremely successful career in the Canadian Air Force as a senior aircraft maintenance engineer. After thirteen years of service I decided it was time to leave the military and move into the private sector; I felt I was still marketable, and not stale from too much time in uniform.

Surprisingly, and in retrospect suspiciously, my job hunt went remarkably well. I quickly found a company that seemed to offer the perfect balance between customer and personnel liaison, and technical expertise that I was looking for. I hung up my uniform and joined a workforce that had me contemplating what I would wear every day from there on in.

My first crack at employment in the private sector was boldly interrupted with an unexpected layoff after a very short six weeks. Needless to say I was devastated and, though I was not the only one to be laid off, I had a difficult time not taking this turn of events personally.

I found myself wondering if leaving the military had been a wise choice. Not being one to ever look back, I started to think that this might be the perfect opportunity to reinvent myself or better yet, to build on what was already a pretty strong foundation of skills.

I was born in Spain to a long line of Spanish ancestors. Even after my family's move to Canada in 1975, we conserved our language and culture while adapting to our new surroundings.

After being laid off, I found I had plenty of time on my hands to reflect on my heritage as well as my military career and I soon realized I'd unearthed a gem. Not only was I fully fluent in Spanish but I'd already taken advantage of plenty of opportunities to hone my skills as a translator and interpreter.

As Canada's military involvement with Spanish-speaking countries increased, I had been frequently called upon to participate in international high-level conferences and bilateral negotiations throughout Central and South America.

I was also selected to be Canada's first female United Nations Military Observer for a UN Mission. The operation in Guatemala in 1997 was tasked to oversee a cease-fire ending a thirty-six-year civil war. My involvement included disarming guerrillas as part of the peace process.

Reflecting on the highlights of my thirteen-year military career I soon realized that I had developed first-hand knowledge and experience with the various cultures of the Americas as well as critical keys to successful business etiquette. It was with these skills that I felt something good was about to take shape. And I would call it Si! Everything Spanish.

To make it work I felt I needed a sound plan. Historically, I have always been one to make plans, even though I have learned over and over again that making plans doesn't necessarily mean they are going to work out. Case in point, I'd planned to be happily married by 25 and to have had all my children by 30. Instead, I was a childless divorcée at 28. But when you're given lemons you've got to make lemonade. And, I am now happily remarried and expecting my first child at 34.

> Believe in yourself, skills learned, ability to plan well, counting on friends, family, networks, and build a solid contingency plan.

I am certain that the discipline and the leadership skills I've mastered during my military career – particularly while attending university at the Royal Military College – will help me to ensure that my business will be the success that I want it to be. (Being a control freak helps too!)

And, by offering a broad range of services and products, doing public speaking, and watching for market opportunities as more and more companies expand their business horizons to include Spanish-speaking countries, I look forward to growing my company and become increasingly successful.

This contribution is ©2005 Lira Martinez of Si! Everything Spanish, and is used with permission.

Never Give Up Your Dream

Heather Resnick

My dream was to move people with words. However, my path towards journalism veered. Fear of failure had enveloped me and, too soon, I abandoned my dream.

Instead, I married and worked as a paralegal, until I had my son, who was followed by my daughter three years later.

Twenty years, I stayed home – a wife and mom. Parenting seemed all-encompassing, exhausting, yet exhilarating all at the same time. It had taken over my life. I needed something to elevate my self-esteem.

I often wondered if I was the only mother to feel this way. I connected with similar-minded mothers and a year later, we had successfully started a parent-child resource centre. Achievement was delicious.

But I was still on a journey to find myself. What did I want to be when I grew up? At first I thought teaching. I had trained as a tour guide for the Anne Frank area at the World Exhibit. I had moved some girls to tears and that led me to believe that perhaps I could become a high school teacher, making the world a better place by teaching today's young people.

So I went back to school to get my B.A. For five years I loved learning, but I struggled to keep focused and it was my husband who encouraged me to keep on track. Almost at my goal of teaching, still working on breaking into the educational world, my life veered again. I was diagnosed with breast cancer.

Cancer was a shock. The fear was consuming. My children still needed me. The surgeon reassured me that my cancer was contained and so they did not check my lymph nodes. I had faith in my doctor's diagnosis and had a lumpectomy and radiation that summer.

In the fall, I graduated on the Dean's List with honours. I took the year off before I applied to the Faculty of Education. I volunteered in the secondary school, ran Girl Guides and spent time being a mother and wife, until I entered Teacher's College.

My first assignment in the classroom full-time was a tremendous disappointment. I was almost 45 and I had no patience for students who had little interest in learning and they seemed typical of my class. Defeated, I relinquished my dream of changing the world through education.

At this point, I was depressed. I'd had a persistent cold and, within months, I developed an oval shaped rash under my arm and three months later, a lump appeared. The cancer was back, and I was angry. Angry that my lymph nodes were never checked. Angry that this meant more surgery and chemotherapy this time.

But life goes on. Three weeks after surgery, my daughter's Bat Mitzvah was held. I was committed to proceed with the celebration. I danced at her party. I recovered a year later, cancer-free, and grateful to be alive.

And like an old friend, I turned to my writing to help get me through this phase in my life. I wrote about being a cancer warrior, about having humour and hope and that summer two articles were published. I felt I had won a lottery!

Finally, my career as a writer was beginning, but I lacked guidance and self-confidence. Although I had the two articles published, I wasn't sure if I wanted to write freelance or work for someone else, and at close to 50, I doubted that anyone would want me. I also lacked strong computer skills. It took me five hours to learn how to indent, but I was so proud of myself when I mastered the skill!

Like many women who had been out of the paid workforce, I lacked technical skills and confidence. I found an employability course for women who had been out of work for an extended period. (I thought twenty years qualified.) The course confirmed my love of writing. I found that the skills I had learned through all my past positions and my personal life could be applied to other things.

The positive encouragement I gained from this course propelled me to take more courses to hone my writing skills. I landed an editorial intern position for a national home and garden magazine. However, I did not want to work nine-to-five or work for anybody else.

Freelance writing for magazines was a slow-going process. It took a very long time for editors to respond to article submissions, and then only some were published. It was not the rejection so much, as the feeling of wasting time.

But I am getting there and will shortly be taking a short-term contract as the interim managing editor at a Web site for a women's organization. Just further proof that we find opportunities around every corner in the road on our journey towards our personal definition of success.

It was a self-publishing course for non-fiction that convinced me that I could write a book. After forty years of telling myself I couldn't or shouldn't write, I now had the gumption to pursue my dream.

By writing about women, falling down, veering off track, struggling to deal with the various roles we have and the challenges we face, and yet still finding a path towards where we need to be, I hope to help empower women.

I want to encourage women to pursue their dream careers, no matter how many twists and turns their path takes. Because I know, eventually if you stay true to your vision, you can get there.

This contribution is ©2005 Heather Resnick, Author, and is used with permission.

ॐ ॐ

Seizing Opportunities

ॐ ॐ

"Instead of waiting for an opportunity to find me,
I decided to find the opportunity!"

Deborah Dennison

Reinventing Yourself

Deborah Dennison

Thirty years in business is a long time! As I look back I can't believe I packed in so much. In a nutshell, two kids, five dogs, two husbands and 15 businesses! I think I have mastered the art of 'reinvention.' And here is my story…

At first I thought opportunities seemed to find me. However, on looking back, I see that I was always open to new opportunities and pretty good at regrouping. For that I have to thank my grandparents, who set the example for me long before I was born.

It started back in the 1930's. My grandparents were poor like everyone else during the depression, so there was very little money for toys. Being resourceful, my grandfather 'borrowed' my grandmother's ironing board and framed it with wood from the coal bin to craft a very rough looking table-top hockey game. My grandmother crocheted a couple of nets and my granddad added some wooden pegs for men. It transformed into a game that would provide many hours of fun to their kids, my dad and his brother. It would also change the course of all of our lives to come.

Opportunity knocked one day, when a peddler came to the door selling baskets made from old records. My grandmother invited the peddler in for a meal, and it all began. The peddler was fascinated as he watched my dad and his brother furiously playing table-top hockey and he encouraged my grandfather to make more and sell them. Granddad took this advice and with all their savings, he was able to put together three games. He gave one to the peddler and took one to Eaton's Department Store leaving it on consignment with the buyer. Before he made it back home, the game was sold. Our family was in business!

Twenty years later, during school breaks, my brothers and I were always expected to work in the factory. We grew up understanding the life of small business. We knew about living with deadlines, supplier demands, and cash flow shortages. And, we were always testing toys, toys, toys. It was an exiting environment and I knew I wanted to be an entrepreneur myself.

The first opportunity came as I was working my way through university. I was a waitress in a fledging pizza restaurant, with an innovative concept – a thin crust pizza cut into squares! Sounds absurd but Sir Pizza became very popular and my new partner (and husband) franchised the concept.

We successfully operated the business for fifteen years, expanding it, adding several new restaurants with different themes, and always striving to stay ahead of the latest trend in the fickle food service business. However, with the sale of the business came the end of my marriage and I found myself a single mom with two young children.

I lost ten pounds, felt much disoriented, had bouts of panic, insecurity, you name it. These were not feelings that I liked. It was time to go in a new direction and try to find my equilibrium again. I decided to first get my career back on track to regain some sense of stability. I took inventory. I knew I wanted to be my own boss, but not in the hospitality business – too frenetic. This time I decided to do things differently.

Instead of waiting for an opportunity to find me, I decided to find the opportunity! It seemed smart to look at things that I really enjoyed to see if a business idea could emerge.

With that in mind, I went on a bit of a journey. I loved greeting cards but had a tough time finding funny ones, so teamed up with a partner to create Bottom Line Cards. Since I was single, I started a dating service, one that helped people meet while driving their cars. (Don't laugh, it's true!) And on it went, exploring each opportunity, starting a business, operating it, selling it and for various reasons, moving on. Counting back, the businesses total more than 15, including an athletic and fitness club, an air charter service, book writing, gift baskets and more. All the businesses had varying degrees of success and each one brought new challenges and lots of satisfaction.

Today, I own two successful businesses. EduService Inc. provides workshops to inspire others to start their own business. DisAbilities Plus assists adults with disabilities, to get jobs or start businesses. Best of all, I love what I do.

What have I learned? Many lessons. Number one, it is important to do what you feel passionate about, what your gut tells you is right. You will be working hard and it's a lot easier when you are having a good time. Number two, listen to the market place. For example, when people say, "I wish…" or "Why isn't there…?" it means a possible opportunity to start something new or expand your direction. But best of all, I learned how to continually reinvent myself. It takes courage, it does not always feel comfortable, and yes, it seems stressful at times.

the courage to succeed
Inspiring stories from enterprising women
103

Here's how to do it…

- Be ready to reinvent yourself: Do this by becoming adept at spotting the signs, i.e., in business, always look for customer demand or market demand, and get excited when changes happen.
- Don't go it all alone, it's tough, so find a partner, a buddy, a role model or a mentor.
- Maintain a wicked sense of humour. I try to find the funny side to every situation and it has been a real life-saver.

What lies ahead for me? I'm sure I am going to reinvent many more times, especially now that I've got the hang of it! Thirty years ago, I did not imagine myself doing what I am doing, or enjoying this life style. It is with great optimism and anticipation that I go forward, knowing it will be exciting, rewarding and – best of all – fun.

This contribution is ©2005 Deborah Dennison of EduService Inc., and is used with permission.

Going with the Flow

Sue Warden

What you see, is what you get. Sue Warden has worked hard not to get caught up in the ego power trips that can overtake TV personalities, and remains down-to-earth and matter-of-fact about all that she has achieved.

At this stage in her life, she'll laugh and tell you: "It takes a lot to live with Sue Warden. I'm driven, all over the place, and a multi-tasking perfectionist. I'm so lucky to be married to Martin, a man who does not like the limelight, but is happy watching me do my thing. My success over the years has given him great pleasure."

Clearly Sue's family keep her grounded, as does her upbringing in a small community where her parents still live in the family home. Her parents have been a big influence in her life. It was her mother, who, true to that era, insisted she take a secretarial course on leaving high school because with typing she could always find a job. And says Sue, "She was right."

Sue stuck out one year of the two-year college program, but when she landed a summer government job in the local courthouse and was asked to stay, she saw no reason to go back to school. After marrying for the first time, she moved into Toronto and, following a short spell with a legal firm, landed a job in a stock brokerage firm. At that time, this was a hot industry, and Sue proceeded to take her Canadian Securities Course and got her license to trade.

When she and her first husband parted ways, Sue moved out to the suburbs where she met her second husband, Martin. After the birth of their son, she lasted three months back at work. "It just was not compatible with motherhood. I worked long hours and never saw the baby," shares Sue. "So we packed up and moved north, three hours out of the city so I could afford to stay home."

It was in this rural community, that Sue launched her first business. "I loved crafts, and I knew I couldn't sit still for too long. I needed to follow my passion." She created a line of Victoriana home decorating products, which she sold at craft shows. Soon she was approached by storeowners and became a part-retail, part-wholesale operation, also dabbling in direct mail. The company grew and did well for five years.

However, there was a family crisis, which resulted in the family moving back to the city. After pretty much losing their house and funds being very tight, Sue was faced with some tough decisions. Should she continue with this business, which was doing well and had a following, or start something new? Her concern was that while the Victoriana trend worked well in the country, it might not meet with the same success in the city.

So, as Sue would say, "It was time to reinvent myself." Through her second business she started teaching crafts in the workplace, people's homes or club settings. It was like a home party business, but crafts. At the same time, Michaels was coming to Canada, and opening its first two stores in the area.

Thinking that this would be a good opportunity to learn more about manufacturers and product, Sue approached them and was hired on the spot. Her responsibility was to get their classrooms up and running, hire instructors, plan the monthly calendar, set up displays, and familiarize herself with the products. "I was the educator, but at the same time, I was educating myself," observes Sue.

Michaels was quickly opening stores across Canada, and Sue spent much of her time travelling across the country, helping event co-ordinators set up their craft programs. "It was a wonderful learning experience. I realized that I loved birthing new projects, and at Michaels that was my job." She got her introduction into the television industry when she appeared as a guest on the Lynette Jennings Show.

After being the guest on different shows, she was approached by Life Network to host her own craft show. In that first year, they shot 120 shows, five shows a day. "I didn't have a clue," admits Sue. "It was a massive learning curve."

Sue ended up hosting as well as creatively directing eight seasons of CraftScapes. "It was a fabulous experience and I feel very fortunate. Although it all sounds very glamorous, it's hard work. Each episode required a lot of research and preparation, but the end result was totally worth it. "

"Surround yourself with good people," advises Sue, "and treat them in the manner in which you want to be treated." It was when she was at Michaels that she first met Kim McIlwaine, who is now her close friend and Creative Manager. "We made an agreement that if it wasn't working, the business relationship would end, as our friendship was too important for us to lose."

Together, along with a very talented group of industry professionals, they have shot 450 CraftScapes shows.

By the beginning of the seventh season, Sue was getting restless and wanted to do something different. She started to write and produced two books, and turned one into her next TV show – Creative Décor which went daily and has since been syndicated into the United States.

And if that wasn't enough, in between all the TV shows, she managed to author a third book. "Writing books is different. When you work on creative projects all the time, you assume everyone can follow you, but when you write, you realize that it's important to give directions in simple language so the projects are doable," comments Sue.

Despite her hectic schedule, Sue has found time to be the celebrity spokesperson for a local shelter. "I feel strongly about domestic violence. It's important we support these women and especially the children, as they are in such vulnerable positions." Through her involvement, the shelter has been able to raise more funds and she finds a great sense of satisfaction in making a difference.

Finding balance is an ongoing challenge for Sue. "I'm guilty of driving myself," she shares, "and I have to make sure I don't run myself too hard." She's tried to set up some boundaries for herself, such as closing her office doors at a certain time but, she realized as we talked, she just moves her laptop to another location. Clearly a work in progress!

Spending time cooking and going to the movies with her husband helps her to relax, and she works hard to stay connected to their seventeen-year-old son, who is quick to give her a reality check from time to time. She also values her relationships and tries to stay in touch with friends.

Sue didn't always have a home office and, in fact, she feels her move to set up an outside office was a mistake. "I'd always dreamt of having my own office, with a sign on the door. I saw it as a symbol of success," she confesses. In reality, it was only a money drain, and it took her away from what she loved to do. "I got caught up in administration instead of focusing my talent, on what I do best."

Assess your financial situation before you move out of a home-based office into commercial space. Do your research with respect to expenses, and hire the right people to help you make decisions.

Sue has always been very good at knowing when to reinvent herself and move on. "I think most of my success to date has been because I was prepared to open the window of opportunity. I would know something was going to happen, and I became proficient at going with the flow." She also has a very positive outlook on life, but admits when she's having down days, "I stay off the phone and try to be on my own."

Life is once again changing for Sue. This year, she became a part of a well-known, U.S. based company – Beacon Adhesives – as their spokesperson, working with them to introduce their product in Canada and expand in the U.S.

Right now, Sue feels there's something else just around the corner, waiting until she's ready to take on a new project. Knowing her, there will be. So stay tuned, and watch for Sue, because her star is still soaring.

This contribution is ©2005 Sue Warden of Sue Warden Visualmedia Inc., and is used with permission.

ဆ �‌ ‌

Letting Go, Moving On

ဆ ‌

"So, for those who believe that they can't get what they want, I'd say: Yes, you can!"

Heather Bordo

Give Yourself Permission to Be You

Heather Bordo

In 2003, I turned my life upside down.

Within a six-month period, I left my husband of seven years, sold my suburban home, spent a month travelling in Europe, moved to a condominium in central Toronto, quit my job as an internal consultant for a media company, and started my own coaching and consulting business.

There is no doubt that all the changes I initiated made for a challenging year, one that I was not sorry to see come to an end. And yet, my experience led to an invaluable learning process that opened my eyes to a wealth of personal and professional insights.

What prompted me to initiate such major life change?

It started in January, 2003, when I participated in an experiential course to formally develop my skills as a coach. One of the exercises we were asked to do was to imagine ourselves twenty years into the future, and to think about what we needed to do to get from where we were then to where we saw our future selves.

The exercise was a huge wake-up call for me. It made me realize that twenty years would pass in a heartbeat and that, if I continued along the path I was on, I would never get to where I wanted to be by then.

I had been living my life the way I thought I was supposed to – the way I thought my family and friends and even society wanted me to. While on the surface it looked like I had it all – a nice home, a good husband and a corporate job for which I was well compensated – but I was miserable.

I had done such a good job of creating a life based on all the things I thought I should do and be for everyone else in my life that I had completely lost myself.

I had lost sight of my values, my passions, the impact I wanted to have on the world, and the person I am at my core and most want to be. I realized that, to really be myself, I had to shed others' expectations, listen to my heart and give myself permission to just be me.

Looking back on where I was, I realize how far I've come. Given the same circumstances, I would make the same decisions all over again. My experience – both in realizing I was unhappy and in initiating a number of changes to resolve my unhappiness – has not only made me a better human being, it has helped me to get much clearer on who I am, what I want and what impact I want to make on others, personally and professionally.

If I had to characterize what I've learned in five key points, they would be:

Know yourself
What are you passionate about? What values are most important to you? What impact do you want to have on the people in your life or on the world?

Take the time to reflect on the answers to these questions and what they reveal about you. In considering what work was most meaningful to me, I realized that what I truly loved about coaching and consulting was the impact I could have on the people I worked with by challenging them to think differently, to see different perspectives and to achieve even more than they ever thought they could. This understanding has led me to be selective. I only pursue and accept work where I believe I can make a powerful impact.

Be yourself
Many factors influence how we behave and who we let ourselves be. Some people feel that being themselves, particularly if it is not consistent with what others (partners, children, parents, friends, work colleagues) need or want from them, makes them selfish in some way.

I would suggest that being anyone other than who you really are does not do you or anyone else justice and, sooner or later, will catch up with you.

I know that I am at my best when I can challenge and be challenged by others, let my sense of humour and sometimes sarcasm show, and not constantly edit my thoughts based on concerns about how people will react if I'm honest in expressing them.

Having my own business means I can be myself without worrying about organizational politics. The people who are drawn to work with me are those who value the very characteristics that make me who I am, which leads to strong, authentic relationships with my clients.

Recognize that you have choices

People who feel stuck in a particular situation, be it an unhappy marriage or a frustrating job, can get quite good at citing all the reasons why they can't make a change. There may, indeed, be lots of good reasons not to quit. However, it is important to recognize that making the decision to stay in your job is your choice.

Resigning from my job and giving up my regular income was a tough and risky decision. However, considering that one of my strong values is living a passionate life, the personal cost of remaining in a job that shut me down felt much greater than any short-term financial sacrifices I would have to make.

Change the way you think

We often limit our own choices by engaging in black-and-white thinking. So, we might assume that our only choices in dealing with an unfulfilling job are to stick it out or to quit.

And yet, there are numerous options in-between that may include taking a leave of absence, taking a vacation, switching to a part-time role, moving to another role in the same company or contracting your services.

The question I asked myself was: What would I need to do to make it feasible for me to resign? I was able to negotiate an agreement with my former employer that allowed me to work my way out of my job over a three-month period while I began to establish my own business. By considering a wide range of options, difficult choices can become more manageable.

Follow your heart

One of the greatest lessons I have learned is how wonderful it feels to do that. For me, this has meant creating a vision of what I want for my business and my life and trusting my own ability to realize it.

Since working internationally is part of following my heart, I participated in a coaching conference in Europe in 2003 to begin to establish international contacts. The conference led to a speaking engagement in Geneva, and I am currently pursuing other opportunities to expand my reach and impact.

I've seen many people dismiss their wishes, dreams and desires before they even give themselves a chance to think them through. I also interact with many people who, like me, have lived much of their life in their head.

So, become aware of what really fuels your soul – you may have to quiet your rational mind temporarily to do that – and consider your options for how to bring that to life.

Am I there yet? Definitely not! But I have made huge strides in rebuilding my life in a way that reflects who I am and what I most strongly believe in. It is amazing, the confidence and sense of fulfillment that comes from being true to me, my values and my passions.

So, for those who believe that they can't get what they want, I'd say: "Yes, you can!"

Living Life Forwards

Anne Peace

On the day I was born, my mother was rushed to the local hospital, where she gave birth to twins. Only one baby was expected.

We grew up in a rural community and when Liz and I were 12, our 16-year-old brother John died of kidney disease and so did a part of our mother and father. Mum never was at peace with a world that gave her an extra baby and took one away.

Graduating from high school with top grades, chosen as valedictorian by my classmates, and runner-up to Miss United Appeal and Miss White Oaks, my sister promptly nicknamed me 'Miss Perfect.' So, why did 'Miss Perfect' suspect that she was 'Miss Guided?'

Pursuing a degree in nursing, I was separated from my sister for the first time. It was there that I realized that I thought of myself as half of a whole. I was alarmed. Being away from home freed up my mind and helped me move away from some of my family's repressive thinking. It also opened up a Pandora's box.

Other thoughts started to emerge. Who did I think I was anyway?

The common child-rearing wisdom of the day was to not raise children who thought a great deal of who they were. The fear was that they might become conceited. Well, my mother was successful. I remember her saying, "Stop your crying, you have nothing to cry about." And, thinking about that one still makes me cry. "It could be worse" was the answer to our need to talk about our problems.

Officially, my answer to all of this lack of connection to myself and to my family was to get my degree in nursing. My unofficial answer was to get a degree in marriage. I married a doctor. Can you see the white picket fence?

The night before I was married I knew that I was not ready but rather than call off the wedding and give all the great gifts back, I went through with it. Eighteen years later, I had two children and a depression that wouldn't go away. It became impossible to live one more day where I wasn't being honest to myself. I had to be brave.

I started remembering when I was a very young child. My mother laughingly would tell her friends that I would make a party out of going across the street. My music teacher wrote in my autograph book: "It isn't often that God gives a child as lovely a disposition as yours, treasure it always."

Everything was a song to me and I delighted in being alive. I would build forts in my mother's country kitchen and in the woods. I played hockey with my sister and our friends on farmers' ponds, staying out all day and coming home laughing. Where did that child and that spirit go? Well I was going to get her back, and get her back I did!

There were many actions that brought me home to myself.
For years, I equated liking myself to some sort of ego-infested wasteland that would lead to terrible things like self-aggrandizement, bravado and obnoxious behaviour. I now know that none of this is true. Liking yourself can be simple and is essential. Therapy helped me with this and my own determination to believe in myself. I broke a cardinal family rule: "Don't ever talk about what goes on in this family, outside of the family." I continue to break this rule. So, strike me dead.

Fast forward to January 2004...
I am 54 years old and have decided to start my own business. After successful careers in parenting, public health nursing and as a teacher of Early Childhood Education at Sheridan College, I was ready to work for myself.

That fear which drove me to an early marriage was back. This time I was going to be brave and loving to the child and adult in me, who, although scared... still sings, plays, believes in herself; loves and trusts with all of her heart; and believes in others with the same ferocity. I realized that I feel lucky beyond belief. I am alive. The message in the movie *The Princess Diaries* inspired me, in that courage is not the absence of fear but rather the judgment that something else is more important than fear, and the brave may not live forever but the cautious do not live at all.

I was going to live.
I took some courses on running a business, joined the Company of Women, and figured out what I love to do and what I am good at. No more power to the voices saying, "Who does she think she is?"

My surname has gone from Ferrier to Sheppard to Peace. Now in a happy and honest marriage, with confident, independent and loving adult children, I formed my company, People at Peace. (No, I am not stuck in the sixties.)

I believe that self-knowledge is a key component for career and life success. I know that it sure helped me. I now work with the tools of personality and temperament theory to support individuals and groups, helping them learn and understand their own temperaments and personality patterns and those of others. I believe that this knowledge will help all of us to accomplish great things and to enjoy peace of mind.

I have given birth to my creative, risk-taking, imperfect self, who cares to focus more on her own needs and less on the opinions of others. I have learned that I am not perfect and that to take risks that may lead to failure, is far better than the protective cocoon I had been so good at spinning for myself.

Letting myself experience how good I am at what I do, and charging appropriate fees to reflect that, has been freeing.

Most of my life I have felt like a plaything of fate. Not anymore. Soren Kierkegaard once said, "Life can only be understood backwards but it must be lived forwards." I am living my life forwards. Can I tell you how wonderful that feels?

This contribution is ©2005 Anne Peace, People at Peace, and is used with permission.

Salute Your Magnificence

Grace Cirocco

My friend Caroline and I were out shopping one day when we noticed some items on a half-price table. Immediately our eyes went to a stunning Serafin angel that had been marked down. I picked it up and noticed a label: Broken – half-price.

Though we looked carefully, we couldn't find the flaw. We took it to the counter and asked the sales clerk to show us the break. She too could find nothing.

"Maybe it was put on the table by mistake," I said.

The clerk went to the back room to ask her manager. When she finally returned, she said, "My manager said that if it's on the half-price table, then it's on sale."

"What about the break?" we asked her.

"My manager says if it's marked 'broken.' then it's broken. Do you still want it?"

"Yes, yes, we'll take it."

Were you labelled 'broken' at some point while growing up? Were you humiliated and dumped on a half-price table for all to see? Were you awkward at something? Not good enough? Too much trouble? Did some adult calculate your worth and give you a price tag? Those labels are rubs on your rock of self-esteem.

Sometimes we may feel like broken angels, but we're not really broken at all. There's nothing wrong with us, but the labels from the past are a heavy burden. We've convinced ourselves that they were right after all. Those labels bruised our spirits. They were the voice of authority that as children we felt we couldn't challenge. But you can now.

Appreciate that you are unique. Even your flaws and imperfections are unique. Connect to your spiritual genesis, to the fact that you have wings. Your magnificent core cannot be harmed by anyone. This is what esteeming the self is all about.

The Tibetan people have a traditional greeting. When they see each other, they put their hands together palm to palm, fingers pointing up, in front of their chest, bow and say the words "Tashi deley." The words mean: I salute the magnificence in you. Imagine what a kinder, gentler world it would be if everyone greeted each other in such a holy way. Tashi deley expresses a deep reverence for one another. It is what our world needs today. It would help us realize who we are if the people around us would, at least on occasion, reflect our magnificence.

When we're not seen for whom we are, we disconnect. We mourn. Remember that when you put yourself down, whether consciously or unconsciously, you are denying your magnificence. And when you deny your magnificence, you give others permission to do the same.

If we become aware of our hurts, learn to feel our pain and heal it, we become whole again. And when we're whole, we feel worthy. When we're whole, we can afford to give our love unconditionally. When we're whole, we don't see the flaws in the angel, we just see the beauty, the magnificence.

This contribution is ©2005 Grace Cirocco, Speaker and Author of Take the Step, the Bridge Will be There (HarperCollins 2001), and is used with permission.

Transition

Janet Auty-Carlisle

Transition seems to be a key word in my life. Diagnosed at the age of 40 with Parkinson's disease, I began a journey that was to bring me almost full circle nearly a decade later.

My first encounter with transitions was through work, when I was a relocation consultant helping people settle into a new community and find suitable accommodation. The job required tact, diplomacy and a great deal of patience as I supported people transitioning into their new setting. I loved the job and every day was a new challenge. I felt very much in control of my life! Of course that's when reality steps in to remind us that we are not infallible.

When I was first diagnosed with Parkinson's disease, I started on the obligatory medications immediately. I was still able to work and, in fact, was offered an opportunity to become one of three partners in my own relocation company.

Almost immediately, I sensed an issue with one of the partners and tried in vain to address it. Always follow your intuition, because one issue led to another, and six months later, I had to leave the company due to irreconcilable differences. I was devastated but had no choice. The company lasted a few more years before the two other partners had a parting of ways and had to dissolve the partnership entirely.

Having to leave the company was a blessing in disguise, as the medications were beginning to have an effect on my motor skills making everyday tasks difficult to accomplish. I enjoyed working in the relocation industry and so, after I left the partnership, I began research for a book project.

Two years later, the first of my self-published Relocation 101 guides hit the shelves. There are now four cities in the series, and we continue to sell them very successfully through the Internet.

The same skills I used to help people through the transition period of moving allowed me to help others with Parkinson's disease to transition through their new circumstances. And volunteering with a local Parkinson's support group strengthened my determination to help myself and others through raising funds for research and support.

I joined forces with a support group leader to co-ordinate a weekend-long education awareness conference for people with Parkinson's and their care partners. It was at one of these weekends that I met the doctor who would provide me with a second opinion on my diagnosis. And, several months later, he reversed the diagnosis, attributing my symptoms to a virus and the stress of the untimely death of my mother-in-law. Looking back, he was my saving grace.

Now, the first time my husband and I heard the words, "You have Parkinson's disease," we were absolutely shell-shocked. I am sure it took at least a year for us to acknowledge that our lives were forever changed. We had made many plans that could no longer be counted on and those wedding vows 'in sickness and in health' were about to be sorely tested. But we adjusted, we accepted, and we got involved.

So, when we heard the words, "You have been misdiagnosed; you do not have Parkinson's disease and you never did," we were absolutely dumbfounded. We didn't know what to say and so said very little. We simply left the doctor's office and drove home. Sometimes shock takes a while to set in, particularly when the news is life-changing. Such was the case this time. And, again I found myself at a point of transition in my life.

We told our children and the rest of our family and friends. The words just didn't seem to be real. How could I have Parkinson's disease one day and not have it the next? Sometimes I felt like I was going crazy during this period. I knew that I should have been feeling grateful, and I most certainly was, but I was also confused and angry. How could our doctor have been wrong for so many years?

For quite some time, we had been asking if the diagnosis was correct and we always received the same response from the Parkinson's specialist, "You're in denial, learn to deal with it." Time was always an issue with our visits. I was always asking questions and getting the feeling that I was being too needy, too pushy. Well, I learned – be pushy if you have to be.

While relieved, my husband was also very angry and he felt we should be compensated. But, on seeking legal advice, it would seem that we did not have a sound legal case.

It took a full year to wean myself off of the powerful drugs I had been taking for the disease. And, at 48 years old, I had a new lease on life. I also had an opportunity to learn from this experience and apply this new philosophy to the rest of my life.

It may sound like a cliché but I truly don't sweat the small stuff anymore. I enjoy my family time and there is plenty of it. My children have learned that there is more to life than 'stuff.' We spend a lot of time together – just enjoying a meal or hiking or playing music.

My firefighter husband has learned to let go of the anger. It took great strength to move beyond the anger and to realize that the change in diagnosis was a blessing. And, we wonder sometimes if this was more about the lessons we still had to learn, rather than a mistaken diagnosis.

Be pushy if you have to be. Doctors are only human and they can make mistakes too; this is your health and it is your right to search for answers.

Some call it a tragedy; still others wonder why I'm not angry anymore. But Parkinson's disease forced us to re-evaluate our goals and future plans for the better. We are much happier now than we were before and our priorities and goals now better reflect what we truly value.

Moving forward from here… I am taking yet another path in my career – speaking to groups as an inspirational speaker and transitional mentor. I am happy to share my story with others, in the hopes that they too may find what it is missing in their lives and reconnect with themselves and each other.

And while I don't know where this journey will take me, I do know that it feels right and that I am headed in the right direction.

ॐ ॐ

Overcoming Life's Hurdles

ॐ ॐ

"Again, I had been reminded that the most important and defining events in life are often outside my control. In this, one of my lowest points, I instinctively decided to just handle what was immediately in front of me."

Terri Smith

Our Role in Life

Terri Smith

Some little girls are born into wealth and to loving parents who wanted and planned for them. I was not such a child. Other little girls are born with great gifts of intellect or talent. These children have interests and desires so well developed that their lives and careers are defined while they are still children. I was not such a child. Some teenage girls are focused and disciplined, and they move through high school with grace and purpose. Before leaving school, they establish the foundations they need to build successful lives and careers. I was not such a girl. Some young women fall in love with strong and wealthy young men, get married and live happily ever after. I was not such a young woman.

No, my birth marked a crisis point in a frightened and shamed young Jamaican girl's life. My mother was the middle daughter of a poor subsistence farmer, and the family was disgraced by my arrival. I was not a pretty child, nor was I born with obvious talent or intellectual gifts. I was a plain, lanky and lazy child, who no one wanted on their team. The only interest that I had, apart from reading a copious number of books, was climbing trees. I was raised by a grandfather who did not like children and a grandmother too tired to show affection to the bunch of us.

But long before the phrase 'just do it' became well-known my grandmother, Mama, drove that message home to me. She would not listen when I complained or whined about my lack of skills, talent, beauty or money. She would say: "You will get only two free rides in life, the one to deliver you to the world and the other to take you to the grave." She convinced me that no one was obliged to like or help me.

Between the ages of 12 and 14, I went to evening classes and I studied to write the Jamaican national scholarship for one of the very few spots in a high school. I won that scholarship, and the entire village was proud. Then by the time I was little more than fifteen years old, I was pregnant and dropped out of school.

My future looked just like that of the majority of young girls in the little villages in Jamaica. The same day my grandmother found out that I was pregnant, she packed me up in the middle of the night and shipped me off to the other side of the country, where no one that knew the family would ever see me. My grandfather would not have to face the disgrace, and I would face my pregnancy and the birth of my son alone.

So, when I had the chance to emigrate to Canada eight months later, I left the baby with strangers and took the opportunity. Six months after I arrived in Canada, I married the first boy who asked me, applied for permanent status, and returned to Jamaica to collect my son. By the time I was 23 years old, I had given birth to three little boys and adopted one, for a total of four sons.

Thus, it was not noble motives and great ambitions that would govern my actions and drive my life. The two driving forces that have motivated and shaped my character, my life, and my business interests are fear and need. More compelling than the desire to do something worthwhile with my life, is the fear that without financial resources I cannot feed my sons or protect them from subtle discrimination or overt racism. I am terrified that if I fail to provide them with a credible role model or if I fail to set the bar high enough, they will resort to designing their lives based on the images of black men presented to them by the mass media. So every time I trip, or fall, or get off track, I sort it out and get back in the game.

By surrounding myself with a very talented and well educated staff I had built a very successful training company. Working with government, educational institutions, and the hospitality industry, my company was very successful in implementing job-related programs. By 1994, I had built a company with over six million dollars in signed contracts. One year later, the government changed and they cancelled programs. Immediately, my clients began cancelling their contracts, and the bank soon seized control of the company and all my personal possessions.

In fast motion, I was bankrupted, homeless, unemployed and in the middle of a very unfriendly divorce. In a blink, I had gone from being a successful employer to an unemployed thirty-six-year-old high school dropout. It was fear that kept me focused when I was often overwhelmed and frustrated. It was need that drove me to get a formal education.

My schedule in the first year at university was brutal. I worked in a factory making sandpaper belts for eight and a half hours, picked up my sons from school, before rushing to classes where I spent six hours, five days per week, all year, including summer. I would spend most of the weekend in the library trying to understand and catch up on the mountain of work it took to carry a 140 percent course load. By the time I had the 22 credits I needed for a B.A. Honors Degree, I was totally exhausted.

The creation and building of AAT School is driven by both a personal and a community need. Three of my children have 'recognized learning disabilities.' My twin sons were born prematurely and suffered with ADHD and other learning disabilities. Like me they dropped out of school as teenagers.

Rick Marriage, a champion of youth literacy and my friend, compelled me to look at the reality for those students struggling in the system. His dream was to build a special school for 'square pegs.' A school where students who were struggling in or who had dropped out of traditional schools could learn how to love learning, rebuild self-esteem, find career focus and earn a high school diploma. I shared his vision, so I convinced my husband to borrow against everything that we owned, and raised the money to build the school. It was an ideal situation.

I would spend the next several months convincing the government to give us full accreditation, while Rick worked long hours nurturing the few students and teachers we had. By the summer of 2004, word had gotten out about us and everything was going fine. We had grown through the worst of the start-up pain, and we were now starting to hold our own.

Then, on a Thursday afternoon, July 22, 2004, Rick went home and emptied his cupboards of all the fun things to eat that he could find. He brought them back to the school, so that the school's snack cupboard would be filled. And, I was really touched by yet another wonderful act of kindness from Principal Rick. So I jumped up and I hugged him for always being so nice. He smiled and walked down the hall and into one of the classrooms. And, suddenly, right there he had a massive heart attack. My friend, my partner, the centre of it all, died instantly.

I had it all planned. And, Rick dying was not on the schedule. It wasn't supposed to be like this. What was I going to do? Everything I owned and cared about was tied up in the school. How were we to keep going when the principal, the co-founder, the heart, the teacher extraordinaire, and the man at the centre of the plan had died?

Again, I had been reminded that the most important and defining events in life are often outside of my control. In this, one of my lowest points, I instinctively decided to just handle what was immediately in front of me.

A week after he was buried, I reopened the school out of an awesome need to keep busy and help my school deal with our shared grief. I was, and I remain, afraid of the enormity of the responsibility of the expectations for our school. But, finding solutions to address needs in my life and in my community captures my imagination, and helps provide focus to my life.

By harnessing the power inherent in my fears, I am driven forward. I do not focus on the image in front of me. Instead, I keep working towards what I am capable of becoming, in spite of my fears, and out of need.

This contribution is ©2005 Terri Smith, co-founder and Principal of A AT School, and is used with permission.

The Juggling Act

Ineke Zigrossi

When Ineke Zigrossi launched her art gallery twelve years ago, she had no idea that fate was about to deal her a full house. Within a year, Ineke and her husband became parents to quadruplets.

"Plenty of people suggested that I give up the business when the babies were born," laughs Ineke. But she wanted to keep her new business alive and achieve balance between her life as an entrepreneur and her role as a mother. If time is any measure of success, Ineke has met her goal. Ryan, Blake, Julia and Derek are now ten years old, and Ineke is still keeping all the balls in the air.

How does she do it? Ineke is a calm, soft-spoken woman who, as she puts it, "doesn't freak out easily." Her even temperament and quiet determination have helped both her business life and her family life thrive. And, she contends, she could not have continued working at all if not for the flexibility offered by operating her own business.

It all started in 1993. Ineke held a senior position as Director of Employee Development and Communication with a large national grocer. Motivated by a fascination for the world of fine art and the help of a friend in the business, she left the world of employment to go it alone. Besides exhibiting contemporary works of art, Ineke decided that Abbozzo Gallery would provide a complete range of services including home consultation, delivery, installation and appraisal. Her business philosophy?

"Go big or go home." Little did she know that this approach would soon overlap to her efforts to start a family.

Because of difficulty conceiving, Ineke and her husband tried in-vitro fertilization. After her first attempt, she 'nested,' sitting very still in a calm environment, thinking good thoughts and hoping the embryos would implant and grow. No luck. Shortly after her second attempt, Ineke had no choice but to travel to Italy for an art show. Ironically, hauling luggage through airports and attending gallery parties did the trick, and pregnant she became. All four implanted embryos grew, and her children were born small but healthy during the sixth month of pregnancy.

With the help of round-the-clock nursing care, the next year was manageable for Ineke and her husband. Two babies came home after six weeks, then the third at two and a half months. Her daughter, Julia, came home last, needing special care for breathing problems. It was her easy-going nature that helped Ineke cope with first-time multi-motherhood. "Routine and structure made all the difference in managing home and business," Ineke explains.

If routine became her best friend, so too did the personal time she has carves out of each day. "The kids have always had an early bedtime so I get at least an hour at night to unwind," she says. Ineke also wakes early to enjoy her newspaper and coffee each morning, and everyone understands that this is her time alone. "I maintain my personal equilibrium by beginning and ending my day with time to myself," she explains.

Still, keeping her energy up and her guilt in check are constant challenges for Ineke. There are never enough hours to do everything she wants to do, both at home and at work. Her hopes to grow her business and attract more established artists are balanced against the needs of her kids as they grow into the teen years. But the perks of self-employment help because the gallery opens at 10 a.m., so she is able to spend every morning with her kids, enjoying breakfast together and seeing them off to school.

Ineke has no regrets, and feels that working at her own business has contributed to her family life in many positive ways. The life she has woven, including her busy home life and challenging outside endeavours, is rich and full. And the kids? They have proclaimed Ineke "a cool mom." And there is no praise higher.

This contribution is ©2005 Ineke Zigrossi of Abbozzo Gallery, and is used with permission.

Work Your Passion – It Will Work For You

Katherine Taylor

I was counting down the days and marking them off on my wall calendar, like a prisoner getting ready to be released. It wasn't the long commute, the constant overtime or even the extremely heavy workload; I just knew that I had to get out before something terrible happened to me. I was very good at my job as a financial billing analyst and loved working with my customers and my peers, but my internal value system wasn't being met by my career.

I wanted to go back to my original passion – event planning, organizing, design, fabric and colour. My children were grown – my time had arrived. When I discussed my decision with my husband, he couldn't believe that I would give it all up – the money, the benefits, the profit-sharing and pension plan. He wasn't happy. The retirement package idea was not really well-received by my employer either, but I could see the writing on the wall and knew like so many, my time would also come. And it did.

I had made four goals: start a business, return to school, do volunteer work and rest. I think I missed the last one. Oh well, we have an eternity to rest. Live each day as your last – right! I had it all planned, I would, for once, invest some money and time in ME.

I'd signed up for some volunteer work at the local hospital, enrolled in a management certification program and was looking for some part-time work until I got my business up and running.

However, despite my plans, it didn't work out that way. My parents and in-laws were starting to need more and more help and a lot of my free time was devoted to them and their needs; who else, after all, I wasn't working! Then my husband lost his job. There we were, both of us unemployed. But he soon found a job making more money than before, and I pursued my dream of owning a business.

Through a chance conversation, I met up with someone who was planning to sell his wedding decorating business. We negotiated a price and I started tagging along with him to assist and learn in preparation for taking over the business. During this time, I hired a valuator, got a business loan for $40,000 and hired a lawyer to complete the deal. The non-competition clause, in retrospect, was an issue but very necessary. I think my business-sense spooked him a little. I believe he expected a friendly handshake deal and no paperwork.

At the same time, I was also chosen to participate in an entrepreneurial program. The next six months were full – as I juggled my time between learning how to run a business, and coping with the rapid deterioration of my father's health and moving my mother into a retirement home. And then my father died and the business deal fell through. The owner said it was taking me too long to close the deal, he didn't agree with the non-competition clause and basically he had changed his mind. Looking back now, I realize that watching my Dad slowly die made this blow seem minor in the scheme of things, but at the time I was devastated.

My parents have very much influenced who I am. Dad always inspired me. He was a visionary and very creative, while my mother is a positive person who attracts people wherever she goes.

By now the time was ticking at the entrepreneurial program. I had to move on but I was still physically and emotionally drained by the loss of Dad. My counsellor was so supportive and really encouraged me to take the plunge, and go it alone. She gave me the courage to take the risk, to believe in myself and my talent, enthusiasm, determination and business knowledge. What a gift she gave me.

With a family wedding on the horizon, I got my opportunity to decorate and with my first wedding under my belt, I booked a booth at a bridal show. My creative juices were flowing and so was the output of money to pull all the ideas together!

I had given back the $40,000 to the bank and then asked for $20,000, so I had money to work with but it was scary. I paid a small fortune for my gazebo which was part of my booth, and I just prayed that the investment would pay off. I seemed to constantly rely on friends to transport me and my equipment around as I only had a small car at that time. It took me twelve hours to set up and I dragged family and friends to help staff the booth. Now that's devotion!

The response was awesome and the first day I secured my first client. Interestingly, the person I was going to buy the business from showed up and was totally blown away by my display. I was gracious and friendly and after that, he passed on referrals to me when he was too busy to take them on.

After my bridal show, I questioned myself. Am I going to play around with this or am I going to run a business? After all the messing around, with various friends helping me with my equipment, I went out that

the courage to succeed
Inspiring stories from enterprising women
143

day and bought a van. This was a sure sign; I was now taking my business seriously.

> Just talking to people has changed the direction of my life. Never be afraid to have a conversation with someone, find out about them, tell them what you are doing; you never know where it will lead.

It has been hard work, challenging financially sometimes, but I just kept plugging away and believing I could do it. There's an ebb and flow to the wedding business, so you have to be ready for the lean times. My husband was downsized once more and is now working for much less income but is happy, so life is good. We always say, "Whatever happens, it will work out."

I have a good solid advertising strategy in place, including a Web site, and I network on a regular basis. I have the good fortune of having a dedicated, hard-working and committed staff that I appreciate, and who have helped make Taylor-Made Memories what it is today. I am blessed with a loving and supportive family and circle of friends. And I give back when I can by supporting charities and mentoring other women in business.

I have continued to do the trade shows and have won best booth twice. I've had steady growth each year, as a result of building good relationships with clients, suppliers, other wedding service businesses and venues. This year alone, Taylor-Made Memories will have completed 131 wedding contracts. And, best of all, is working with the brides to make their day special.

This contribution is ©2005 Katherine Taylor of Taylor-Made Memories, and is used with permission.

శ్రీ రా

Succeeding
in a Man's World

శ్రీ రా

"You've got what it takes! Hard work and a lot of faith will always pay off in the end. But, it will never just come to you, you have to want it, and then go and get it."

Karen Hatcher

Challenged by Change

Debbie Gracie-Smith

"We used to meet in each other's homes, usually picking the person with the largest dining room table!" chuckles Debbie Gracie-Smith, co-owner of CRATOS. "Little did our first client know that we'd just rented a boardroom for our meeting, but it didn't matter, we landed the account." Today, her company hires close to 50 people around the world, and occupies 16,000 square feet in its own building.

> Follow your passion. Be prepared to work long hours and harder than you have ever done before.

Debbie has come a long way from her early days working as a receptionist at a local real estate office. Today, she is ranked #56 among the top 100 Canadian women entrepreneurs listed by PROFIT magazine. And as a woman in the male-dominated IT industry, she truly is a pioneer.

As the oldest of five children, her parents had a strong influence on her life, inspiring her to be whatever she wanted. And she's followed an indirect path to get there, from working as a receptionist, a typesetter and a government bureaucrat to managing a major IT project for an international corporation.

It was when she was working at a community college that she realized that she needed to go back to school. She took a two-year intensive course, condensed into twelve straight months, in computer programming, and hasn't looked back since.

Five and a half years ago she started CRATOS Technology Solutions Inc. with three other partners. They had no financing, and used their own funds to get the business off the ground. And now even with revenues of $7.2 million, they still pay themselves last. Two years ago, she started CRATOS Integrated Solutions Inc with her current Technology business partner and two others.

Two of the partners from Technology Solutions have since been bought out and the two remaining partners are now running the company. She's found there are some distinct advantages to having a male business partner. "There are some countries, like Japan, where it is culturally not good business to make the clients deal with a woman," observes Debbie. "You can't take it personally and just have to let it go."

> Financially, make sure you have enough money to cover your costs – business-wise and personally for the first six months, as money may be slower coming in than you expect. Try to get a line of credit early on.

So what exactly does CRATOS do? There are two arms to the company: one that specializes in credit card software for several financial institutions, with clients in over 15 countries, as well as North America; and one that builds software for the hospitality industry, customizing menu screens for restaurants, with handheld wireless devices for taking food orders. Within their building, there's a mock restaurant where clients can test out the software first hand.

Getting to this stage in the business has not been easy. Financing was the biggest challenge. "None of the banks wanted to look at us." Debbie shares, "although maybe now that we've reached a certain level, they might consider us."

Keeping staff motivated, challenged and current has also been an ongoing issue and one that Debbie is responsible for as she handles all the human resources within the company.

What has made the business successful? It's a niche market and with their flexible work arrangements, they have been able to attract and retain some of the top people in their field.

Start your customer relations early. It's always a juggle between growing the business, doing the work and keeping the customers happy, but customer relations are important.

Provided with laptops, their consultants can work remotely. With the use of technology, they could be working in another country, at home or outdoors. All of which is reflected in the company's overhead costs and their ability to attract people who need and enjoy the flexibility that the company has to offer.

These work arrangements lend themselves to stay-at-home mothers. It is therefore not surprising that 60 percent of their staff are women, which is unusual for an industry that tends to be male-dominated. "They can work whatever hours suit them as long as all our deadlines are met," advises Debbie.

Her three teenaged sons can certainly attest to the hours their mother puts in. "I think it's good for them to see that work is not always a regular day, and that if you want to get ahead, you have to be prepared to work hard," shares Debbie.

Originally from Nova Scotia, Debbie retains her down-to-earth, common sense approach. It's her sons, she adds, that keep her grounded as only teenagers can do, and while the business has been successful, she takes just as much pride in their accomplishments.

Like many women, she is juggling the demands of work and family and she has a hectic travel schedule across several continents that often keeps her away from home.

When asked why she had joined Company of Women, Debbie was quick to reply, "I wanted to get a life. My time is spent between work and family, and I needed to do something for me."

This contribution is ©2005 Debbie Gracie-Smith, CRATOS, and is used with permission.

Don't Stop Believing!

Karen Hatcher

When I was asked to write the piece for this book, I was extremely honoured. I was in a room with the group of women that you are reading about right now. We were all asked to tell a little about ourselves. As I sat and listened to these incredible women and their stories of how they got from A to Z, I was in awe.

Their stories were filled with every possible human emotion, from the feelings of failure, hopelessness, and personal strength... leading to great success in all their respective fields. My eyes filled with tears a few times during that meeting. We all exchanged cards, numbers, e-mails, and hugs for sharing such heart-to-heart stories. I came home and thought all night long, "What should I write?"

My name is Karen Hatcher; I am a thirty-six-year-old mother of two beautiful children, Josh and Jessica. They are my life, my inspiration, and my driving force to be the best I can be.

Presently, I am an electrician and network cabler. I am the owner and CEO of Kennedy Electric & Cabling. Lately I have been receiving much attention for my successes and endeavours as a business woman in a male-dominated field – the skilled trades.

As women, we all sometimes feel that we are not worthy of praise or compliments, we never give ourselves credit for a 'great job.' We just DO IT! Now, I want you to go make yourself a cup of tea, get in your comfiest pyjamas and I'll tell about the 'Amazing Rollercoaster Ride of Karen Hatcher.'

It all started in 1968. I was born to Rose and Brian Kennedy. I was child number three, between two older brothers and one younger brother. My parents were amazing bringing us up; they were very young and we didn't have much, but we were always happy to be together. We fished, camped, played, laughed and danced all the time.

When I graduated from high school I had no clue as to what I wanted to be. My father, a triple-ticketed electrician was transferred to another city and my brothers and I had to make the choice between following our parents or staying where everything was familiar. I decided to make the 'big move.' I started working at my dad's factory as a summer student. I was 18 years old and my plan then was to take a year off and decide what exactly I was going to do for the rest of my life. I was one of only five women in a factory of 160 employees.

I was married at 24 and a young mother of two kids by 28. I was EMPLOYEE 084 – nothing more, nothing less. I was extremely unhappy and dissatisfied with my job; I always felt I wanted to do more with my life. These feelings led to depression and extremely low self-esteem. I felt like a robot: punch-in, punch-out, come home, cook, clean, read bedtime stories, bath and then bed. Every day the same thing!

My marriage and family life disintegrated over the fifteen years of working at that place. I couldn't snap out of it. I felt like I would rather stick a needle in my eye than walk through those factory doors one more day.

I was at a crossroads. I looked into a university education and was very disheartened to realize that the expense of a four-year university education was not in the cards for me. More depression and I entered another relationship, which turned out to be an absolute nightmare.

Completely alone with the kids again, I had no money and no possibility of any kind of future for them or me. You can imagine the thoughts going through my head at that time. I felt beaten down, I didn't want to get up ever again.

Two months later, after being a complete zombie, I was in the living room looking for some pairs of socks so my kids could go to school. I was staring at the basket of socks searching for a pair; I couldn't find a match, not one. I started shaking and crying. My little girl picked out a pair and said, "Mommy here's a pair, don't cry anymore, it's okay." It hit me like ton of a bricks, I grabbed them both and hugged with all my strength and told them how sorry I was for everything. I told them, "We are going to be alright, I promise."

I had over fifteen years of factory experience. I was over-qualified for entry level jobs, but under-qualified for skilled jobs, so I was offered retraining. As a young girl, I used to take apart toasters, much to my mother's frustration, so the skilled trades seemed a good choice. I took test after test, and electrical kept popping into my head. My dad is an electrician; my brothers are all in the skilled trades… why not? In March 2003, I was accepted in an electrical and network cabling pre-apprenticeship course. I was the only girl in a class of 16 men. I was excited and nervous at the same time. School – I hadn't been in a classroom for over sixteen years.

It was extremely hard at first getting used to the homework, studying and being a mom at the same time. There were lots of extremely late nights cramming for exams and practical tests. The guys in my class all became my brothers. I was like their 'cool mom.' We all helped each through the hard times and did study groups together.

There were times when I felt I just couldn't do it anymore. But, then I would walk into to my kids' rooms and look at their little faces when they were sleeping, and knew within myself, I will do this!

All my fears, and sometimes tears, paid off. In November 2003, I graduated with Honours from that course. I started working as an apprentice right away. I couldn't wait to start. In February 2004, I started my business, Kennedy Electric & Cabling. I named it for my Dad, who is my hero. Tears rolled from his eyes when I showed him my Masters Business Licence. And, that's how it all started…

As a female electrician, in a male-dominated field, I have heard it all. When anyone first meets me as I walk up to their home or worksite, they say things like, "You're the electrician?" I have heard comments like, "Isn't there a height requirement for electricians?" or "Do you need a ladder to get to your ladders?"

I never let any negative comments get to me, not anymore. I know my job and I know my field. When people, usually men, make comments like these, I just smile. Then, they see me work and they realize pretty quickly, that I am efficient and very professional. I have earned the respect of male electricians, inspectors and related fields. They all call me 'Smiley' now.

I received the Mayor's Award of Excellence for New Entrepreneur. The business took off. I felt like pinching myself every day… Is this real? I have been in the newspapers, asked to teach women electrical work, and I even got to meet Don Cherry. I do a lot of guest speaking, and my message is always believe in yourself and never give up hope.

And there's more to the happy ending. I met a man, Kevin Firmage, I call him 'my newfie,' and he is absolutely wonderful and extremely supportive. Our family now is six, his two kids and my two kids and he and I… Brady Bunch style. If you have ever felt like there is no hope, think of your friendly neighbourhood, 5'1" female electrician, who kicked her own butt and beat the odds.

We all have it in us. When you're lying on the ground feeling down, GET UP, dust yourself off, hold your head high and show them all. You've got what it takes! Hard work and a lot of faith will always pay off in the end. But, it will never just come to you, you have to want it, and then go and get it.

This contribution is ©2005 Karen Hatcher, Kennedy Electric & Cabling, and is used with permission.

ဆ ၵ

Staying the Course

ဆ ၵ

"In today's economy, running a successful family business for thirty-three years, speaks of determination, tenacity and vision. It speaks of strength of character and it speaks to success."

Anne Day

The Tira Factor

Julia Hanna

The life of a restauranteur is often glamorized but I recall a truer description of this life, attributed to an accomplished restauranteur – Dominique Chapeau...

It's a wonderful life, if you can take it. A restauranteur must be a diplomat, a democrat, an autocrat, an acrobat, and a doormat. He must have the facility to entertain presidents, princes of industry, pickpockets, gamblers, bookmakers, pirates, philanthropists, popsies and a ponders. He must be on both sides of the "political fence" and be able to jump the fence...He should be or should have been a footballer, golfer, bowler, and a linguist as well as have a good knowledge of any other sport involving dice, cards, horse racing and pool. This is also useful, as he has sometimes to settle arguments and squabbles. He must be a qualified boxer, wrestler, weight lifter, sprinter and peacemaker.

He must always look immaculate – when drinking with ladies and gentlemen, as well as bankers, swank people, actors, commercial travelers, and company representatives, even though he has just made peace between any two, four, six or more of the afore mentioned patrons. To be successful, he must keep the bar full, the house full, the stateroom full, the wine cellar full, the customers full, yet not get full himself. He must have staff who are clean, honest, quick workers, quick thinkers, non-drinkers, mathematicians, technicians, and who at all times must be on the boss's side, the customer's side, and must stay on the outside of the bar.

In summary, he must be outside, inside, offside, glorified, sanctified, crucified, stupidified, cross-eyed, and if he's not the strong, silent type, there's always suicide!"

If you think this sounds slightly exaggerated, come spend a week with me!

My first vivid memory of the restaurant world was as a 20 year old, working part-time at the front desk of a prominent hotel, while going to school. It was 7:30 in the morning, and I went to the massive hotel kitchen to make myself some toast. This kitchen was on fire with activity. The executive chef, who to this day is a member of the elite, and his team were hurriedly preparing for a very high profile lunch when out of the corner of my eye I caught the chef's knife flying across the room, a busboy ducking out of its way, and it embedding itself on the kitchen wall.

I went running to the general manager's office screaming for him to call the police and have the chef arrested. What I didn't know was that while I was trying to get the chef arrested, the busboy was apologizing for getting in his way. And, the only reason I kept my job was because chef found my reaction highly amusing!

Yes, it was and is a very different world, this restaurant business! Statistically speaking, nine out of ten restaurants close their doors within the first three years. I am not aware of what the figures are for manufacturing, retail or other service industry, but no doubt many fail. The question has to be why – why go into your own business? Because you want to be and believe you can be the small percentage that succeeds.

The small business world is more competitive today than ever. What does that mean? Does it mean you stay away? No! It means you enter better and stronger. One of my favourite phrases is due diligence – my husband Brian uses that one a lot. It means you must do your homework. It means you pick everyone's brain – lawyers, accountants, friends. It's like pieces of a puzzle, and the pieces have to fit.

But there is one piece that is unique to every small business. It's the piece that is intangible. It's the piece that every successful small business has. Large corporations spend millions trying to create it. It's the Tira factor. Tira is the Italian word for pull. It's that thing that pulls people through your door. It's the relationship and the emotional connection you create with your customers, your guests. Large advertising firms try to create this relationship between their large corporate clients and their customers. Small business owners have it and it is real.

In 1983, I opened my first restaurant, Café Galleria. I was 26 years old, had $328 in the bank, and thought Oakville was so far from Toronto you needed a passport to get there! Just before opening, I was a manager at the hottest restaurant in Yorkville – celebrities walked through our doors daily – it was a very 'chi chi poo poo' place.

But along the way, the owner forgot it was about the guests, not him. I never felt he connected with everyone, only those he thought were worthy. I wanted a place where everyone who walked through the doors knew they mattered – a place I would feel at home. Café Galleria is where I first began to learn the dance of the small business.

As in any dance you have two partners – these partners are dreams and reality. You begin your business with dreams leading the dance, but it is ultimately reality that takes the lead, but that's okay because that means your dreams can continue to dance. After selling Café Galleria in 1993, I had a dream of a Mediterranean restaurant.

I know that 'passion' is an often overused word and unfortunately an underused emotion but I wanted to share this passion for this exciting cuisine. Within our first year of opening Paradiso, we had a couple dining who had just finished their meal and were leaving the restaurant and asked if we would consider hosting the Juno party.

I looked at this gentleman and his wife who sat at our best table on Friday night and had two cranberry juices, a bowl of pasta and a pizza. He was wearing a fish t-shirt, and said he was the President of Sony. Sure, and I was the Queen of England! Luckily he had a sense of humor because on their drive home his wife said, "She doesn't get it."

I just couldn't believe our good luck – it was the server who treated them as if they had ordered the finest bottle of wine and a chef who made the pizza that reminded them of Italy. They were made to feel welcome and they wanted 150 people – many of Canada's finest recording artists – to have the same experience. We held the Juno party three years in a row until they moved it to Halifax. But that's what business is – opportunities gained and opportunities lost. If we had not had the Tira factor that night, we would have never known what we would have lost.

Fear of failure and fear of change seem to immobilize us at times. They are an inevitable fact of life. After four years, we had the opportunity to expand. We opened a take-home, meal-replacement food shop called Nonna's Mercato. Customers loved the reasonably priced good food to eat in or take out.

But, I ignored one very important rule of business – location, location, location.

Customers needed to be able to get in, pick up their food, and get out quickly. Anyone tried doing that at a busy downtown site? I learned much from that experience, especially when I shared it with others in business who reassured me that a failure in business is part of doing business. We turned Nonna's Mercato into a cooking school and started our Corporate Team Building that we continue today at Julia.

How do you measure success in business? It isn't just about the money. I'm not naïve. If it isn't a monetary success, you won't be doing it for long. It's about your quality of life. If your business is making money, but at the cost of your family, friends and your health, that is too big an investment for any business.

It's the incredible cast of characters you work with. It's about the people you meet – not just the celebrities. It's about the young girl with the purple hair who worked with us when no one else would hire her. She is now a marine biologist in Hawaii and comes to see us every year.

It's about the young boy who, as a child, would only want one thing to eat – fettucine alfredo. And, as a young man, had a horrible car accident. It's the joy you feel when you hear he is out of the hospital and the first place he wants to go is to your restaurant and have a bowl of fettucine alfredo. It's watching his mother's face light up watching her son eat. That's when being in business is really sweet.

The Reluctant Entrepreneur

Kathy Thomas

Back in 1971, Kathy Thomas would probably have described herself as the reluctant entrepreneur.

She was 22, had three young children, including a six-week old baby and no serious income. It was her husband, John, who had the burning desire to start a landscaping business. Having just lost his sales position through downsizing, he was hesitant to get back into that arena. So he ran an ad in the local paper and took the bus to his first contract.

The early days of Green Thumb Landscaping were tough. Kathy was running a boarding house to bring in some extra income and when John landed a townhouse contract with 33 units, she had to help out. One of her boarders looked after the children, while she went to work with John.

Very much a hands-on learner, she took courses and read books on accounting and bookkeeping, so she could manage the business's finances. By 1979, the business was booming and they had 40 employees. Then the recession hit and they were back down to eight. All the time, John, ever the salesman, was thinking up new schemes, and Kathy stayed steady, keeping the business and family anchored.

Some would say that they balanced each other out well, but by 1984 Kathy wanted to sell the business. She'd had enough and wanted to grab back a life for herself. John didn't sell the business, but Kathy embarked on a new career, one that she enjoyed and to which she found she had a talent. It was her first real job and for several years she spearheaded several programs to help youth find employment and to assist welfare recipients starting a business.

"I finished my grade 12 by correspondence, so it was a surprise to find myself in the role of educator. It made me realize I had learned a lot over the years – about hiring staff and running a business," shares Kathy. "I really felt I was making a difference and that was important to me," she adds.

All the time that Kathy was gainfully employed, she was still doing the books for the business at weekends and evenings. "It was a demanding, stressful time trying to balance it all." she admits.

> While you need a plan when you start a business, whether it is on paper or in your back pocket, you need to be flexible, light on your feet and ready and willing to change direction in order to succeed.

In 1992, Kathy was asked to start the Entrepreneurial Development Branch of the local business advisory centre, a new pilot program being launched by the government and she welcomed the challenge. For the first nine months, all was going well and she saw record results from her efforts. Then her world changed.

John, at 48, died of a heart attack. Kathy found herself a widow at 44, with three daughters, a business, and a career to juggle. Suddenly she was the sole owner of the business she had never wanted to start.

For a while she tried to manage both her career and the business but it was clear that it was too much, and so she devoted her energies to rebuilding Green Thumb Landscaping.

Over the years, family members have been involved, which added another dimension and dynamic to manage. "It's not always easy, it takes some flexibility on both sides to make it work," she observes.

Today, they have 30 employees and are a vibrant, well-respected landscaping company. Kathy has remarried and eighteen months ago, opened the Bronze Frog Gallery, a downtown retail store. "I've always thought of Green Thumb as belonging to my husband. Opening the gallery to enhance the landscaping division gave me an opportunity to expand my creative side," she explains.

> Surround yourself with people who will support you. We all need mentors in our lives and it is important to give back. If you've learned something, share it.

She researched the concept of art and gardens and feels she has identified a niche market, and as you walk around the store, it's easy to admire the beautiful statues and artifacts she has found.

Next will be an online store so people can purchase items through the Internet and she continues her travels to find unique and attractive curios from around the world.

Kathy Thomas has come a long way from the farm girl growing up in rural Ontario. "We didn't have running water until I was eight. As farmers, my parents never had a regular income. Maybe that's why being an entrepreneur is not foreign to me, I've lived with insecurity all my life," confesses Kathy. "It's my fear of failure that has led to success."

In today's economy, running a successful family business for thirty-three years, speaks to someone with determination, tenacity and vision. It speaks to the strength of character deep inside Kathy that she has overcome the setbacks, the family challenges – to not only maintain the landscaping business – but to open a new one. It speaks to her success.

This contribution is ©2005 Kathy Thomas, Bronze Frog, and is used with permission.

Creativity + Courage

Jean Price

With her spiky platinum hair and infectious giggle, you automatically feel Jean's warmth and energy, but the generous smile belies a life that hasn't always been that easy.

Growing up in the Donna Reid era, Jean's aspirations, when she left school, were to get married, have children and live happily ever after. But, as we all know, life isn't like that. Jean did get married at 18 (not something she would recommend) but it didn't work out.

Her first career goal was to become a legal secretary and she did. Working her way up from file clerk to law clerk in a local lawyer's office, she stayed there twelve years until she decided to move to Toronto.

By now divorced, she moved there with her partner Fred, and managed to land an administrative assistant position at Osgoode Hall. Fred was working as a sales manager at a hardware company but both had a yearning to start their own business.

At the age of five, Jean had learned to sew from her grandmother, and she had always loved designing her own clothes. Anxious to learn how to do this professionally, she enrolled in a local college to take evening classes in pattern making, design, etc.

Clews Clothing grew out of these classes. She and Fred started off running the business on the side. Both worked full-time during the day, and at night and at the weekends, would design and sew the clothes. To launch the business, they held a home party, inviting family and friends to see and sample their designs.

From there, they decided to set up a booth at the One of a Kind Show. "We invested every penny we had in the stock for that show," confides Jean. "We weren't sure how we would feed ourselves that Christmas if nothing sold." But the gamble paid off, and the company made its first money.

For three years, they kept up this double life – employees by day, entrepreneurs by night. It was exhausting. They focused on craft shows and home parties, and word of their designs spread. At that time, they were still taking on every aspect of the business – cutting, sewing as well as sales, but the time came when they had sufficient work to hire others to do the home parties and to help with the sewing.

By now they had to ask themselves whether they were really serious about the business, and the answer was yes. So Fred quit his job, and eight months later, Jean joined him. "Our family just shook their heads. One of them asked why I had given up a good government job with a pension," reports Jean. They just couldn't understand but, by the same token, were willing to help out financially, as the banks were just not interested. The business was considered too much of a risk.

Both were free spirits and determined to make a success of the business and, seventeen years ago, they purchased their existing building – 6,000 square feet – in which they live, work and house their retail store.

Like many retail businesses, cash flow was often an issue. However, it was when the bank phoned on a Friday to call in their line of credit ($30,000) and expected payment on the Monday that Jean realized how vulnerable they were. She managed to negotiate a deal with the bank, and was determined never to have the company placed in such a tenuous situation again. "In many ways, every time the bank turned us down, they did us a favour, because we went ahead anyway and were more creative as a result," observes Jean.

"We often seem to get pushed to the edge, then something would come along," she remarks. Take when they decided to open up a second store in cottage country. Summers were slow in the city, partly because their clients went off to their cottages. To compensate for the slow sales, Jean and Fred had been participating in craft shows in cottage country. But one year they were not selected to participate in what was normally their biggest summer show, and this forced them to think of alternative ways to raise the missing revenue. So they found suitable premises up north. Although turned down by the bank for a renovation loan, they decided to proceed and were able to give the store a fresh look on a shoestring budget.

Creativity is clearly an integral part of their success. Jean's enthusiasm for the business is very evident. "I love the sewing. It is such a unique business. Every six months I get to work with new fabrics and designs, so it is like starting over twice a year." It also takes a savvy business mind, as Jean has to calculate how much fabric she needs and how many outfits she can sell within the sixty to ninety-day turnaround, so the bills get paid on time. "Keeping your suppliers happy is crucial to your survival," she observes.

When asked why women like Jean's clothes, she is quick to tell you that she makes them comfortable. "They're for real people, not models," she responds, "and we pay attention to detail, always using quality fabric." With 75-80 percent repeat business, clearly Jean is doing something right. Rather than being swayed by the colour of the month, she selects colours with her customers in mind. And customer service is important to her. "We welcome customers as we would guests into our home," she adds.

> Find yourself a mentor. I made so many mistakes at the beginning but if I'd had a mentor in the same business, I could have saved myself so much grief and money.

"There's a sense that the fashion industry is glamorous but it's hard work. Few get discovered overnight and many of us put in 'sweat equity' to get ahead," comments Jean. Yet, the business has made it and today with over 10,000 people on their database, Jean and Fred take great pride in what they have achieved.

And so in 2000, it seemed an obvious next step to move to bigger premises in a nearby town. "We were actually looking at space, ready to take the plunge, when the accident happened," shares Jean.

Jean and Fred were hit head-on by a car. The other driver died, and Fred was seriously injured, unable to work in the business for close to two and a half years. When you hear Jean describe their working relationship, it is evident that they enjoy working side by side. Each brought different talents to the business and complemented each other and so you can only begin to imagine the sense of loss and fear that Jean faced as she carried on alone. "I think it was adrenaline that kept me going, but the accident really made us reflect on what is important in life."

Fast forward to 2004, and Fred is back working, but he's rarely without pain, and can no longer stand for hours cutting fabric. But Jean and Fred have a new attitude. "There are no guarantees what will happen next week, so we take the time off now. We travel and take vacations when we can. We've come to realize that our relationship is important – and we need to invest time in each other."

> I have enjoyed mentoring other women for the past eight to nine years. I'm pleased to let people pick my brain because I always learn something too.

Clews Clothing is a business built on creativity, hard work and love. Jean has survived the ups and downs of twenty-three years in the fashion industry which speaks to her tenacity, enthusiasm and dedication to the business, to her customers and to her partner, Fred, without whom, to quote Jean "none of this would have been possible."

This contribution is ©2005 Jean Price, Clews Clothing, and is used with permission.

ಔ ಜ

Giving Back

ಔ ಜ

"When you decide to make a difference in the lives of others it is not about race or colour, but about the desire and the passion you have to make someone else's life better."

Anna Aidoo

A Legacy of Love

Anna Aidoo

"When I die, I want people to say that I was an inspiration machine," shares Anna. Now Anna is a woman with a mission. She is determined, and destined, to make a difference in the lives of women.

"I am just carrying on the work my mother started. I want women to realize their worth, in the same way my mother always encouraged me and helped the people in our community."

Anna was born in Ghana, and raised in a large family filled with brothers, sisters and cousins. Her father did the best he could to raise the family in a comfortable neighbourhood, while her mother kept the family together.

Anna's mother was very aware that others were less fortunate, such as the women who used to carry their produce on their head to sell at the market. Many times, after the family left home in the morning, she would bring them home for a place to rest. They would leave feeling somebody cared.

Hearing this story of Anna's mother, it's not hard to understand why Anna has the same calling to reach out and support others. Growing up, Anna witnessed the results of her mother's endeavours, yet she often wonders if her mother fully recognized the value of her work, or felt appreciated for what she had done for everyone.

Since the age of 19 Anna has lived in both the United States and Canada and has endured trials and tribulations that would have stopped anyone else in their tracks. But Anna continues to find the lessons and jewels that lie in her struggles and to encourage others not to give up.

In May of 1998, Anna's mother passed away at the age of 65. Anna's life then took a drastic turn that threatened to crush her hopes and dreams.

Anna went to Ghana for two weeks to join her family in saying goodbye to their beloved mother. "I had become numb from my mother's death, and also from the fact that I had to live without her," shares Anna. "Nevertheless, I remember how she always told me to be strong and so I kept moving on."

Because of circumstances beyond her control, Anna's life hit an all-time low when she and her children had to move into a shelter. "When I look back at where I have come from and what I have overcome, I knew I had to reach out to those who may be hurting as much as I did back then," she confides, "and I still do hurt sometimes when I think about those times."

Life is much better for Anna now. She and her husband publish *Unique Magazine* which highlights the positive contributions black Canadians have made in Canada. And, in 2003, she held the first *A Woman's Worth Conference* which was attended by 100 women from all walks of life.

Except for some funding from a few businesses in the community, the rest of it was fully financed by Anna and her husband. Now Anna is not a financially wealthy woman, far from it; both she and her husband work full-time to support the family, but she is rich in every other sense of the word and believes in investing her time and energy in others.

In fact, you get the sense that her paid employment is just a necessary means to a more important end, and that her 'real' job, the one supporting women, is the one that rewards her the most.

Her faith in God guides her and she feels she is just an instrument carrying His word. "He gives me the right words to say, so that my message lives in the hearts and minds of the people that I meet."

This journey has brought many surprises to Anna. Support has not always come from those closest to her, but she realizes that everyone has his or her own path, and though it is lonely sometimes, if the goal one is pursuing is genuine, one cannot give up. "When you decide to make a difference in the lives of others it is not about race or colour, but about the desire and the passion you have to make someone else's life better," she observes.

Her courage to lead has also surprised her. She never thought she would be able to do this but each step brings her closer to furthering her goal of helping women believe in themselves and realize their highest potential.

While Anna's mother laid the foundation and gave her daughter a road map to follow, Anna is carving her own route, finding her own way to make difference. It is not an easy journey. There are roadblocks, disappointments and diversions on the way, but there is little doubt that she will reach her destination. And, when she does, there will be many women along her travelled path who have benefited from her wisdom, passion and determination.

Anna is living her mother's legacy – a legacy of love, hope and inspiration.

This contribution is ©2005 Anna Aidoo, Endless Possibilities Group, and is used with permission.

Acts of Kindness

Deborah Seigel

Deborah can best be described as resourceful. She's a person other people call when they need something: be it the right connection, solid information or advice on finding good value. She never disappoints, which is why her phone is always ringing.

Starting out in the '70s in the demanding world of retail management, Deborah transitioned to the wholesale side of the fashion industry as a manufacturer's representative in the early '80s and worked her way up to serving key accounts and training sales teams. In the 1990s, she landed another dream job in fashion as an executive assistant.

By that time, she had met and become engaged to Ron, a caring gentleman whose extensive business experience also included decades of community volunteer service, primarily in the area of fundraising.

By the fall of 2001, Deborah's mother, who had a history of mental illness, was beginning to decline in health. She had been hospitalized on a number of occasions and Deborah, a regular visitor at the local hospital, had become known to the staff and administrators.

As a result of her visibility and commitment to the cause of mental health, Deborah was asked by the administration to represent the perspective of families on the Accreditation Team, as well as sit on the hospital's Psychiatric and Mental Health Services Committee, whose purpose is to enhance the quality of patient care. She whole-heartedly accepted both invitations.

As a social entrepreneur, Deb was seeking a creative solution to the hospital's challenges and was determined to approach them from an attitude of abundance rather than one of lack. Soon, she began to visualize how donations of everyday items and a network of volunteers could make a significant impact.

While attending a women's conference, Deborah was introduced to a woman who was recognized for her 'acts of kindness' initiative and immediately realized that this was the very term she had been seeking to describe her idea. She returned from the conference primed to build a network of acts of kindness. After some initial planning work and talking with friends, she met with administrators at the hospital to share her concept. To her delight, they loved it.

"We developed the premise around a theme of 'community supporting community with time, talent and tangible goods,'" she explains. "We also felt that it was important to invite clients and patients to 'pay it forward' too, by donating an act of kindness as an expression of gratitude for the support they received. The goal was to make them feel part of the community and help them develop confidence and self-esteem."

In October 2002, immediately after the meeting at which the Acts of Kindness Network was approved in principle, Deborah visited her mother in hospital and revealed to her that she had been the inspiration for Deborah's vision and commitment to make a difference in the mental health community.

"Although Mom replied that she'd had nothing to do with it, I made very sure she understood that she was leaving a legacy," Deborah emphasizes.

When her mother passed away two days later, Deborah invited her friends and business associates to memorialize her mother by supporting others with mental illness and donating to the Acts of Kindness Network.

"My invitation was well received and the response was generous," she notes. "The resulting number of donated goods and services we collected was absolutely awe-inspiring."

Before long, Deborah was able to provide support to numerous other organizations related to mental health in the community. Donors are asked to contribute everyday items, such as personal care products, underwear, hats and gloves, games, videos, books and magazines, as well as gift certificates to restaurants and movies.

In addition to its Christmas drives, the Acts of Kindness Network responds throughout the year to the requests of the various mental health organizations it serves.

"One of my goals is for the case managers to never have to personally buy products for their clients from their own pockets as they so often do," she emphasizes.

Like any true social entrepreneur, Deborah has an underlying desire to change society through her work. Improving the public's perception of individuals affected by mental illness is a top priority and she's devised some ingenious strategies to achieve it.

Listening to Deborah speak animatedly about her favourite cause and her ideas for its future evolution, it becomes abundantly clear that she is drawing her seemingly endless energy from an inexhaustible power supply – a daughter's love for her mother.

This contribution is ©2005 Deborah Seigel, Social Entrepreneurs Network, and is used with permission.

৪১ ৫

Courage to Succeed

৪১ ৫

"As women, our lives are like a tapestry, made up of different threads, all woven into the fabric of who we are and who we can become. Through Company of Women, we wish to weave wisdom, warmth and wellness into your everyday life."

Anne Day

Weaving the Threads

Anne Day

I grew up in Scotland and then England, immigrating to Canada with my husband in the early days of my marriage. Looking back, we were taking such a risk as we had no jobs, but we were young, in love, and it seemed such an adventure.

Having my first child opened up a whole new career for me, as together with four other mothers we started a family resource centre in our community. None of us had ever done anything like this before, but we knew first hand that such a service was needed to support parents of young children. For three years, two of us ran the place as volunteers but it was on-the-job training and we learned many skills, and I admit, some the hard way. Later on, it became paid employment, and while I left after eight years, the centre continues today as a vibrant and vital part of the community.

From this grass-roots beginning, I've had a very eclectic career from running a women's centre, working with teen mothers, being editor of a national parenting magazine to working for the government on women's issues. But it wasn't until I was in my late forties that I took the plunge and started my own consulting business. And, to my surprise, I did well.

Like many women, I've discovered that my skills are transferable. No matter what I have done, it has always involved communicating with people, facilitating discussion and then either writing reports or designing programs that accurately captured the essence of what was said or needed. I've often felt like a catalyst, bringing the right people together to make things happen.

Starting Company of Women therefore seemed like a logical next chapter in bringing women together. I am often asked why I started the organization, and if I am honest, initially I rather saw the network as a means to an end. I really wanted to run conferences for women and thought I could draw on the women in the group to attend my conferences.

One year later, have I run one? No. Will I? Only if the women say they need one. That has probably been one of my first lessons in running this group – ask first, listen, and then deliver what people want, rather than determining from afar what they need or what you would like to offer.

At times, I feel as if my entire life has been spent just gaining the skills and experience to run Company of Women, and it is still very much on-the-job learning. At 53, I've found out what I want to be when I grow up! But in looking back, there were some signs along the road that have pointed me in this direction.

Right from the start, as an only child growing up in a household of adults – my parents and grandparents – I was surrounded by love and attention, and encouraged to be whatever I wanted to be. But on the downside, it was lonely and I've often wondered if that loneliness has been part of my driving need to bring people together. It has certainly given me an understanding and insight into how isolated people can feel and how we need to connect with one another.

When I was 39, I got a wake-up call. I was diagnosed with breast cancer. My daughters were young and my biggest fear was that I would not live to see them grow up. But I survived and learned an important lesson – we only have one life and we have to live it to the fullest. Making a difference, leaving a legacy, became important to me and I became more selective in what I did and where I expended my energies.

The next 'nudge' I received was in 1999, when I received the ATHENA Award for helping women realize their potential. At that time, I was working for the government, developing initiatives that helped women get into the skilled trades and young girls to choose rewarding careers.

Receiving this award was a tremendous responsibility. I felt I had to live up to the ideals extolled by the ATHENA Leadership Model and attending my first ATHENA conference was a life-changing experience.

As I listened to a motivational speaker encouraging us to be authentic and true to ourselves, I knew I had to take action. I came back and decided to quit my job. While I learned many new skills and worked with some wonderful, bright women who are friends to this day, I was never destined to be a career bureaucrat, locked in by the restrictions of government. So I cut myself free.

Since then, I have become even more involved with ATHENA, and serve as the second Canadian representative on the board of directors of the U.S. ATHENA Foundation. As a side note, it was the ATHENA conference that I wanted to replicate through Company of Women as it never seemed fair that I could benefit from these inspiring speakers, when so many other women could also grow and blossom from such an experience.

Certainly I never expected the overwhelming response that Company of Women has produced. When I booked the room for the launch, I guaranteed only 35 people. With a turnout of 165 women, that should have been my first clue that I was onto something. By the end of our first year, we had 300 members, and women were coming from great distances to attend the events.

What makes it work? For several months, I have asked myself that same question. I think part of it is that there is a sense of community and connection. The women care and support each other. We are the cheerleaders for each other. One of our speakers once said, "When you own, you're alone." And she was right. Yet, as business owners we face the same issues, regardless of the type of business we operate. We don't have to be alone.

The women who make up the fabric of the Company of Women are diverse, but the threads of their lives have become intertwined, creating a stronger framework upon which we can build our futures and move forward.

I'd like to think we are an inclusive group – not all the women own a business, some are in the corporate sector, others are in transition, not sure what their next step will be, and we have a small group of seniors from whom we draw wisdom based on their years of experience.

Women tell me they feel safe and that there is no pressure to perform, sell or buy. And that, with our inspiring speakers, they leave the meetings feeling motivated, more able to accept risk and take the next steps on their journey to success. Giving back is also an integral part, so we've had the chance to support other women through grants and in-kind support.

What's next? Well, we're looking at taking Company of Women on the road, because whether you live in Vancouver, Calgary or Halifax, women have similar aspirations. We want to provide women with the tools and confidence to achieve their potential, to realize their dreams and – working together – trust me, it will happen.

Postscript to my story…

As we finalize the stories for this book, I receive the news that the cancer is back. After fourteen years, I have to say it comes as a bit of a shock. But as one of my friends once said, cancer is a club to which unfortunately your membership never expires and I guess mine has just been activated again. What does this mean? Well, as I am scheduled for major surgery, I guess it may take us a little longer to achieve our goals for Company of Women, but I am determined that we will.

It has also caused me to stop and ask myself what the lessons are in all of this. Already, I am overwhelmed by the words of love and gestures of kindness by my family and friends – a lesson I learned last time, but a good reminder of how much people care about me. It feels good.

One thing that cancer or any life-threatening illness does is force us to face our own mortality, and how we have to live each day as our last, for who knows what tomorrow will bring.

Having said that, I have no intention of checking out yet, I have too much to do and too many dreams to fulfill. So stay tuned, there are more chapters to unfold in the book of my life.

This contribution is ©2005 Anne Day, Company of Women, and is used with permission.

ಚಿ ಌ

Lessons

Learned & To Learn

& Resources

ಚಿ ಌ

"The way we act and react to our business contacts should be no different from the way we do to our friends and family. Generosity in business, just like in life, it will come back to you."

Marcia Barhydt

About Business

Anne Day

There is an old Chinese proverb: "I hear and I forget. I see and I remember. I do and I understand." Following an amazing first year with Company of Women, I truly understand the challenges and joys of business start-up. Oh, I've had my own business for several years, but as a consultant, you tend to be tied into your client's requirements rather than carving out a niche for yourself. Here's what I understand…

- Listen to your customer. Take your lead from what they say they want, not what you think they need or what you want to sell.

- Be flexible and open to new ideas and prepared to change direction if it makes sense.

- Build a support system. Surround yourself with people who believe in you and give you that extra boost of confidence when you doubt yourself.

- Life happens. No matter how much you plan and organize, external events will happen that can throw you off course or cause delays.

- Step out of your comfort zone, that's how we learn and grow.

- Negative people are often hurt inside. Be patient. Show some care and understanding.

- Go that extra mile to help someone out. Your generosity of spirit will not go unnoticed.

- Seek input. Ask people what they think rather than making a decision in a vacuum. Then they have some ownership in the results.

the courage to succeed
Inspiring stories from enterprising women
195

- Everything takes longer than you think, especially when you are doing it for the first time.
- Give back. Get involved in your community; you gain as much you give.
- Say thank you. No one achieves success on their own. Remember to thank those who have helped you on your journey.

This contribution is ©2005 Anne Day, Company of Women, and is used with permission.

About Life

Nancy Douglas

Doing what's right for you provides balance and time to stop and smell those roses you've been planting, or meaning to plant...

- Committing yourself 100 percent doesn't mean committing 100 percent of yourself.

- Life is all about choice. The balance in your life or lack thereof, is a result of the choices you make.

- Fear paralyzes life. We act like we're living, but we're just going through the motions.

- Unless you're a brain surgeon, at the end of the day, it's just a job.

- Invest in and protect your most valuable resource – yourself.

- Let life consume you, not work.

- Clarify what's really important and be vigilant to allocate your time accordingly.

- It is possible to change.

This contribution is ©2005 Nancy Douglas, Strategic Life Coaching, and is used with permission.

Eight Rules to Guide the Journey

Marcia Barhydt

Rule #1 – Love what you do – have passion for your business. Your passion will help you excel almost automatically.

Gather up your nerve and dive into something new. It's terrifying, but one never knows what one can accomplish until one tries.

Rule #2 – Never, ever, be afraid to try a different approach to a challenge. If it doesn't work one way, try another.

When one method of attack doesn't work, try a new method and keep trying until you find the method that works for you.

Rule #3 – Listen to others when they make suggestions to you. Their ideas are gifts.

You may discover that you have a new found talent that never would have occurred to you.

Rule #4 – Run your business with the morals and ethics that you run your personal life.

Rule #5 – Give your time freely to others and you'll all benefit.

Rule #6 – Keep your competition close – close enough to make them your allies.

Rule #7 – Form a mastermind group only with women you admire, trust and feel totally comfortable. Share everything with them – your good moments as well as your bad ones and really listen to their advice. Their caring will guarantee suggestions that will benefit you.

Choose networking groups that are right for you and, if you realize that a group isn't working for you, look for a new group that might be a better fit.

Rule #8 – See the warning signs of overwork. Don't be so rigid that you refuse to make changes that result in a kinder lifestyle – don't buy into the superwoman.

Have the courage to make whatever lifestyle changes are necessary for you. Your business is not your life. Make appropriate changes as there is no greater achievement than balance and moderation in all parts of one's life.

This contribution is ©2005 Marcia Barhydt of Willowtree Customer Service, and is used with permission.

How to Create a PR Buzz and Get Noticed

Susan Valeri

You've worked hard to get where you are. Your product, service or book is ready for the consumer world and you are preparing to announce it. However, taking some time to plan will pay off in the long run. Decide who your target audience is, and the key messages you want to share with them. The following tips can help you create the buzz you deserve.

Tie your offering to current events

No matter what you have to sell, you need to find a way to tie into the news. With increasing competition from the Internet, movies, and celebrity gossip, it will be hard to get coverage unless you differentiate. Newspapers and magazines are also trimming back their coverage so it has become more difficult than ever for publicists, let alone businesses, to make an impression. That's why the way to make the news is to either become the news, or become an expert commenting on the news. Make use of current trends and statistics.

For example, a book that was mainly about love and intuition got little attention from the media until it was tied it into divorce statistics that made major headlines. Quick action got the author onto television and radio promoting her book, as well as establishing her as an expert.

Know the right reporter/producer/editor

It is a good idea to thoroughly research a publication or show before sending your information. This can be done online or you can watch or listen to the show you wish to appear on. Take time reading the section of the newspaper that applies to your business. Find out the correct person to send your information to and method in which they prefer to receive it. Don't just assume that fax or email is okay. If you are unsure, pick up the phone and find out.

Using a publicist can be like a filter: a professional who understands that not every offering is right for every media outlet. In most cases, the publicist has developed a relationship with the media contact and there is a comfort level already established. This alone increases your chances of coverage.

Get an interview on videotape

This is the backbone of any publicity campaign if you want to get on television. You may already have appeared on local television but, if you haven't, be prepared to start there and get a solid interview on tape. You can request a tape from the station or get someone to tape it from home. Most national television shows will not consider an interview without this tape. If necessary, invest in a media training session to prepare you for the first time on camera.

Patience is a virtue: give it some time

A major market newsroom can get hundreds of news releases every day. Most magazines have lead times of three to six months. Like the fashion industry; when you're on the beach, they are thinking about Christmas. Newspapers are usually the quickest to pick up a story, but radio and television can take a couple of months to book. Production meetings often review your videotape before an interview is scheduled. Follow-up is the key and can result in some quality media interviews for your business. Bookings may come in a flurry and there may be some dry spells. Keeping this in mind can save you some stress!

Prepare a complete press package but avoid gimmicks

Well written press materials that include a biography, news release, product sheet, reviews, articles, show angles and media questions showcase you as an expert. Although there is a lot of competition, you don't want to give editors or producers the idea that your offering cannot stand on its own merit. Using gimmicks may hamper your chances rather than help. A well presented, professional press kit will establish your credibility without screaming desperation. Remember to include it on your Web site for quick access by the media.

Now you are ready to move forward with creating a buzz for your business! Take a deep breath and keep your calendar handy!

This contribution is ©2005 Susan Valeri, The Powerful Publicity Group, and is used with permission.

છ૦ ૦ર

Do You Have What It Takes?

Having what it takes to run your own business includes possessing the personal skills and having a product or service that will sell.

Webster's New Collegiate Dictionary defines an entrepreneur as "one who organizes, manages and assumes the risks of a business or enterprise."

Does this definition fit you?
You need to evaluate your strengths to find out what you have and what you need. The following five activities will help you do this.

First, start by making a list of the personal qualities you think are necessary to be successfully self-employed. Here is a list of personal qualities that many advisors would agree are important.

Write down those that you think apply to you.

- creative
- determined
- energetic
- healthy
- patient
- persevering
- self-confident

- resourceful
- competitive
- flexible
- self-motivated
- ambitious
- intuitive
- organized

Then, list all of your relevant business skills. Here are a few to get you started:

- accounting
- selling
- people
- presentation
- management
- teamwork
- promotion
- computer

Next, consider your special areas of knowledge, achievement and/or interest. These might include things that you feel most comfortable doing and talking about.

From your lists, you may conclude that you lack some of the skills and knowledge to start your business. What are they?

Finally, which skills can be improved and which must you acquire elsewhere?

Remember, you don't personally have to 'do it all' but you are responsible for everything.

Source: Eight Steps to Self-Employment: A Practical Guide for Women, authored by EduService Inc. – Courtesy of Deborah Dennison ©2005 EduService Inc.

Self Employment - Is It for You?

Feasibility Questions
Briefly describe your business idea.

- How will your business idea blend with who you are, your interests, your personality, your experience and your contacts?

- How does your idea fit with the current business trend or opportunity?

- How do you know there is a proven need for your product or service? In other words, what research have you done so far?

- Describe your most likely customers and indicate how you will reach them.

- What are the benefits and weaknesses of the product or service from your customers' point of view?

- Who else is in the business, and is there room for one more?

- How much will you charge for your products or services and how long will it take to make a sale?

- If your business sells a product (instead of a service), how much does it cost to produce the product, not including your labour?

- List the equipment, services, materials and/or training programs required to start your business. Indicate why you need these services or pieces of equipment and include the costs to purchase each item listed.

- What equipment do you have now that could be used in your business (include phone, computer, software, special equipment, skills, etc.)?

Authored by EduService Inc. – courtesy of Deborah Dennison. ©2005 EduService Inc.

Thank you once again to the following contributors, without whom this book would not have been possible.

Contributors

Anna Aidoo is the owner of the Endless Possibilities Group and *Unique Magazine*, aimed at African Canadians.

Pat Atkinson is a communications specialist and journalist.

Janet Auty-Carlisle is the publisher of Destination Canada Publications and has recently embarked on a new career as a motivational speaker and workshop leader.

Marcia Barhydt owns and operates Willowtree Customer Service. Willowtree offers Customer Service Keynotes, Workshops & Training.

Teresa Biagi Gomez designs custom jewellery.

Catherine Bobesich owns Wellness by Design, which offers seminars, speaking engagements and personal coaching. She also represents a line of home and personal care products.

Heather Bordo operates her own coaching practice.

Cathy Boytos owns Trading Places Home Décor which sells fine quality furnishings on consignment.

Wendy Buchanan is the owner of Perceptions Eyewear Inc. She is a licensed optician as well as a trained image consultant.

Grace Cirocco is a speaker and the author of the national bestseller *Take the Step, the Bridge Will Be There* (HarperCollins 2001).

Anne Day is the founder of Company of Women, creating personal and business development opportunities for women.

Deborah Dennison is the owner of EduService Inc., offering self-employment training and other educational workshops, and DisAbilities Plus, a company that finds employment opportunities for people with disabilities.

Christine Desforges is a print and communications specialist, working with Company of Women.

Nancy Douglas operates two coaching businesses – Strategic Life Coaching and Executive Coaching Services.

Debbie Gracie-Smith is the President of CRATOS Technology Solutions Inc. and CEO of CRATOS Integrated Solutions Inc.

Lorraine Green is the owner and operator of Lorraine's Pantry, a catering service.

Carol-Ann Hamilton is founder and President of Changing Leadership and Spirit Unlimited, and author of *The A to Z Guide to Soul-Inspiring Leadership*.

Julia Hanna is the owner of Ristorante Julia, Oakville.

Karen Hatcher is the owner of Kennedy Electric and Cabling.

Angell Kasparian is the President of GRAND Enterprises Inc. and publisher of *GRAND magazine*.

Cheron Long-Landes is the owner and designer of Cheron Dearle Designs Inc.

Eva Martinez is the owner of Si! Everything Spanish.

Mary Ann Matthews is the President of *handwriting.ca* and a certified handwriting analyst (graphoanalyst).

Janee Niebler is a Doctor of Homeopathy, and her company is Homeopathy Life.

Andrea Nielsen owns As it Happens Photography.

Anne Peace is the President of People at Peace.

Jean Price owns Clews Clothing, with retail stores in Port Credit and Port Carling.

Heather Resnick is the author of *Ms. Humpty Dumpty* and currently working on her second book, *Women Reworked*.

Deborah Seigel founded the Acts of Kindness Network.

Terri Smith is the co-founder and Principal of AAT School.

Katherine Taylor is the owner of Taylor-Made Memories.

Kathy Thomas is the owner of the Bronze Frog Gallery in Oakville and Green Thumb Landscaping Services.

Lucy Vandermeer is the owner of Bras by Lucy.

Susan Valeri is the owner of The Powerful Publicity Group.

Sue Warden is the President of Sue Warden Visualmedia Inc.

Heather Wilgar co-founded DietDelivery Canada Inc. with her brother.

Ineke Zigrossi is the owner of Abbozzo Gallery, Oakville.

ଛ ଓ

For more information about our contributors, please check the Company of Women Web site at:
www.companyofwomen.ca

1 The Life of the Restaurateur – The Sanitation Operations Manual, National Restaurant Association, 1200 Seventeenth Street, N.W. Washington, DC 20036-3097

About Company of Women

Company of Women is an organization dedicated to creating personal and business development opportunities for women.

Founded in September, 2003 by Anne Day, this organization has met with outstanding success in its first year of operation. Three hundred women, from across the Greater Toronto Area (GTA) have joined as members and a vibrant Web site has been developed to support women in their endeavours.

Company of Women offers:

- Monthly dinners with inspiring speakers
- Trade shows
- Web site
- Print directory
- Monthly e-bulletin
- Quarterly newsletter
- Group benefits plan for members
- Golf clinics
- Mentoring program
- Access to experts
- Advertising opportunities
- Opportunities to give back and get involved in the community

Plans for expansion are underway. So, if you are interested in bringing Company of Women to your community, please contact Anne Day by email: anneday@companyofwomen.ca

To learn more about Company of Women, check our Web site:

www.companyofwomen.ca

From the Publisher

The definition of success is very different for each and every one of us. One might think that the key is not in defining yourself by someone else's standards or measures, but in discovering your own defining moment, or moments, or series of life events... your success.

This book illustrates how many different women have defined success. We hope that you enjoy their stories.

ℬ ℛ

A special thanks to our amazing partner Anne Day for her vision, endless energy and hard work, and her way with people. And, to Christine Desforges for being a valuable part of our publication team with regard to copy edit and cover design, Anne Peace for keeping an eye on our readers, and to our editorial board for all their work.

ℬ ℛ

TRIMATRIX Management Consulting Inc., under the BEL Learning (Business, Education & Life Learning) publications imprint, works with organizations and educational institutions to develop and publish books that share knowledge and learning, and strive to make a difference in communities and the lives of individuals.

www.trimatrixconsulting.com